Dowsing *Magic*

Book 2

From grumpy gnomes to healthy homes

Grahame Gardner

Acknowledgements:

My thanks to my wife Elspeth (as always), Peter Knight for the foreword, Ivo Dominguez Jr for permission to adapt his divination model, Cherie Lavalle for the element drawings, and Pamela Bailey for proofreading and editing help.

Cover photo: The Lochmaben Stone, near Gretna on the Scottish border.

Dedicated to Patrick and Sig – thanks for the journey.

By the same author:

Dowsing Magic - Book 1
From water finds to dragon lines

A Basic Guide to Technopathic Stress

Dowsing with Sigils (A Dowsing Magic Workbook)

Available direct from:
https://westerngeomancy.org/

Dowsing *Magic*

Book 2

From grumpy gnomes to healthy homes

Grahame Gardner

Dowsing Magic - Book 2
From grumpy gnomes to healthy homes

© 2020 Grahame Gardner

Published by Western Geomancy
Glasgow, Scotland
https://westerngeomancy.org/

Printed by Inky Little Fingers

ISBN 978-1-8380461-0-1

Contents

Foreword

This book is the eagerly awaited sequel to Grahame's *'Dowsing Magic - Book One'*, published in 2012 with a second updated edition released in 2018. Book One explored the basics of dowsing techniques and devices, including rods and pendulums, as well as defining ley lines, geopathic stress and suggesting that we live in a *'conscious universe'*.

Grahame served for many years as President of the British Society of Dowsers and, in this latest volume, brings to bear his wealth of experience as a professional dowser to the subject of house healing, which he presents in his signature accessible style – blending authority with a light touch for maximum readability. Those new to dowsing, as well as more experienced dowsers, will find considerable food for thought in this essential guide.

Practical tips are interwoven throughout the book, and the sections dealing with geopathic stress provide valuable guidelines for living in closer harmony, both with the land and within our own homes. Grahame's insights on 'house clearing' offer ways to improve health and wellbeing through releasing and diverting detrimental energies, drawing on methods such as intent, dowsing, and crystals.

He also guides us on a journey through water divining, as well as into the spiritual dimensions of water, delving into the admirable and ground-breaking discoveries of Dr Masuro Emoto. Water, ultimately, is everything, is life itself.

Further sections profiling shamanism, cosmology, *'dragon energies'* and the spirit of place will resonate with those seeking to develop deeper connections with the land, and with the planet as a whole. As Grahame says, *'dowsing opens doors in your mind'*. As he suggested in Book One, the universe really is a result of the wondrous expression of consciousness, of which we are all umbilically connected. This new volume guides us further down the road of our collective and individual paths. Let the author guide you (clutching your dowsing rod and pendulum as you go), down many paths of revelation, as he convincingly advocates that the world is more miraculous than we had previously perceived, and that we are all co-creators in a conscious universe.

Peter Knight
(Sacred sites guide and author)
http://stoneseeker.net/

Introduction

Sit down before fact like a little child, and be prepared to give up every preconceived notion, follow humbly wherever and to whatever abyss Nature leads, or you shall learn nothing.

-- TH HUXLEY

Before we begin, let's get one thing straight. This book will *not* teach you how to heal your home. No book can teach you that. What this book *will* teach you is how I might go about healing your home. How you would do it is likely to be a different matter entirely, as you have your own values and belief system that are in all probability significantly different from mine. There are many ways to skin a cat, as the saying goes. But I hope that this volume will provide some insights into the geomancer's art, aid you in identifying problems in your own space, and prompt you to develop skills in this area.

This book is not aimed at novice dowsers. Some level of dowsing competence is assumed. You should at least be confident in your use of pendulum and L-rods to get the most out of this book. If you are not experienced, the previous volume *Dowsing Magic – Book One* provides enough basic groundwork to get you up to speed. If you have some dowsing proficiency and are interested in developing your house healing skills, then this book is for you. If you are a homeowner worried about geopathic stress or are concerned about something feeling 'not quite right' in your home, then you will find something here to help you categorise what is going on. But please, consult a professional dowser or geomancer to help you rectify the situation. Healing your own house, especially when you have been resident in it for any length of time, is not an easy task as it is well-nigh impossible to remain objective about your findings – we are all too inclined to overlook minor issues because we have become used to living with them.

There are many books on the market about house healing, yet most of these seem to be based around conventions of space-clearing and de-cluttering in the style of *feng-shui*. The few that are aimed at dowsers generally deal with 'hands-off' healing techniques using focused intent and visualisation. While these can be helpful, I wanted to author a book that looks at the more practical, hands-on, aspects of house healing - those that are employed on the ground, so to speak. However, the book is not just about house healing, nor is it just about dowsing. The first part of the book explores more philosophical and esoteric concepts such as shamanism, magick, the memory of water, the nature of consciousness and reality – ideas that go beyond pure dowsing and are better housed under the mantle of geomancy. Dowsing is merely the tool that helps us to access these areas. The latter part of the book applies these models to the art of healing sick houses.

Dowsing allows us to detect the presence of various subtle earth energies and assess their nature and quality. Some of these energies are related to geomagnetic anomalies created by the presence of flowing underground water, subterranean cavities, mineral and crystal deposits, and geological faults and fissures. Other energies have a more subtle quality similar in nature to the meridians of *chi* in the body found in the practice of traditional Chinese acupuncture. Just as healing of the body can be effected by inserting needles topically at nodal points on these chi meridians, so we can balance the telluric energy networks using techniques of *earth acupuncture*.

At any given location, the earth energies may be beneficial and healthy for human activity. Conversely, they may be detrimental and unhealthy, or neutral with negligible effect on humans; yet those same energies that are detrimental for humans may prove beneficial for some plants and animals. It's a complex picture. Spending prolonged periods of time, either at home or at work, in a place where the subtle energies are unsupportive of human health is a common dysfunction in contemporary society, and the effects of this lead to what is known as *geopathic stress*.

There is a tendency amongst energy workers to focus on finding these detrimental areas, almost to the exclusion of any beneficial energies that may also be present. Yet we must remember that geopathic stress is just one side of the energetic picture. Although dowsers are frequently called upon to remediate these detrimental energies in the already extant spaces where we live and work, they can also locate positive, healing, beneficial energies that are supportive of human activity, and it is important not to lose sight of that. More emphasis is placed on locating these beneficial energies when seeking locations to build spiritually oriented structures like churches, temples, healing centres and suchlike, places where the energies can be supportive to the function of the space. This is a core discipline of geomancy.

Finally, a caveat: The art of geomantic house healing is a large corpus of knowledge to absorb, and I cannot therefore hope to distil all the wisdom that I've learned over several decades of study and working in this area into a single volume.

Healing a house is not a task for beginners, particularly where psycho-spiritual activity is involved. It requires practical, hands-on instruction in order to attain anything like proficiency in this area If you are not already a competent dowser, I recommend that you seek out such training from an established practitioner if you wish to go down this route. Find a local dowsing group if you can, join your national dowsing society and see if they have any professional members near to you, take as many courses and apprenticeship study options as you can find. Also look into related disciplines such as feng-shui, kinesiology, reiki, shamanism, and spirit release for example. These are all complementary and cross-disciplinary where house healing is concerned and competency in one or more areas can be profitably applied to your dowsing work.

Chapter 1

Models, Magic, and Metaphysics

If you want to find the secrets of the universe,
think in terms of energy, frequency, and vibration.

-- NIKOLA TESLA

After consistently practising for some time, most dowsers come to realise that the Universe comprises more layers than can be accounted for by reductionist Newtonian science. It is simply inconceivable that the science we learned at school can explain what we are discovering with our dowsing tools. For instance, as mentioned in *Dowsing Magic – Book One*, even the conventional theory of ground water and the hydrological cycle is incapable of explaining why dowsers can consistently find water sources that lie close to the tops of mountains. For the dowsing community, the answer lies in the alternative theory, put forward by dowsers, that water can be created independently of the hydrological cycle under certain geological conditions. This theory was finally vindicated in June 2014, when a group of scientists, in a paper published in the prestigious peer-reviewed journal *Science*, announced their discovery that a huge reservoir of water, three times larger than all the Earth's oceans combined, exists in a region between 400 and 700 kilometres deep in the mantle, the layer of hot rock that lies between the Earth's surface and the core. Water becomes trapped under intense pressure and elevated temperatures in a rock called ringwoodite.[1] The scientists' findings completely substantiate the dowsing theory of 'primary' or 'juvenile' water, a source independent from the normal hydrological cycle.

This is just one example of the sort of discoveries that can be made when we harness our intuition with our pendulums to seek otherwise unobtainable answers to our questions. But where does this information originate?

The Dowsing Source

When tutoring pendulum question-and-answer sessions, one of the most frequent questions asked by students is, "Where does this information that we are getting come from?" In other words, what is the source of the dowsing response? It's a question that has taxed the mind of every dowser at some point. Do our answers originate from our subconscious mind, or are we connecting to some transcendent external intelligence that is supplying the information?

Let's consider a scale that we might call, for argument's sake, the 'dowsing spectrum'. At one end, we find those dowsers who only search for tangible targets, for example water, archaeological remains, or other physical features, who insist that dowsing can be explained using standard scientific models. This paradigm posits that the dowser is reacting to some disturbance in the geomagnetic (or perhaps the gravitational) field that occurs over the target, and sooner or later conventional science is jolly well going to have to accept this and validate dowsing as a genuine biophysical reaction to these subtle fluctuations. It may even be possible to explain some of the more intangible earth energy dowsing findings as electromagnetic variations. Yet it is much harder to postulate a conceivable explanation for map and remote dowsing as an electromagnetic phenomenon, since there is no possible physical connection between the dowser and the target.

To explain this apparently supernatural ability of dowsers to attune to and receive valid information about a distant location, we have to accept the reality of 'spooky action at a distance', to quote Einstein's condemnatory phrase about quantum mechanics. The more esoteric aspects of dowsing, such as distant healing and the seeming ability of dowsers to actually *influence* reality at a distance – for example in 'calling in' water to replenish a dry well over the phone, or clearing geopathic stress without having to visit a property - forces us to set aside conventional science and look to other disciplines in order to try and explain what our pendulums and rods are telling us. This brings us neatly to the other extreme of the dowsing spectrum, where you will find the intangible target dowsers – those who dowse for earth energies, healing, auras, and so forth.

If such a dowser comes from a religious or spiritual background, then whatever picture he or she draws upon to explain their experiences will almost certainly reflect those same religious or spiritual influences. So, the dowsing response might be attributed as a 'gift from God', although more fundamentally minded people opposed to dowsing are more inclined to brand it a 'tool of the Devil'. This harsher view dates back to the time of the Reformation, when dowsing and other forms of divination were condemned as sin by the Protestant preacher Martin Luther. [2] Other dowsers might ascribe the source of their answers to angelic communication, spirit guides, their Higher Self, or some other supernatural source (or sources). I know of at least one respected dowser who regularly checks his sources to ensure that they continue to be aligned with his best interest and to make sure that his dowsing is accurate.

Alternatively, a more pragmatically-oriented dowser will likely shy away from such quasi-religious models in favour of more rational explanations for dowsing, perhaps looking to some as-yet-unknown mechanism that allows the conscious mind to access and interpret information from the subconscious, and considering the existence of a universal 'information field' from whence the dowsing answers come. As we saw in Book 1, there is a dearth of research to corroborate this line of thinking as such an approach violates the standard scientific model, which has no framework for discussing the nature of consciousness. According to philosopher Philip Goff, we have Galileo to blame for this disparity, as he declared that the *qualitative* nature of consciousness cannot be explained using the *quantitative* vocabulary of science, and thus has to be left outside of the scientific paradigm where reality is captured by mathematical reasoning. Goff writes:

> *When it comes to the basic causal workings of the universe, scientists provide mathematical laws which describe with great accuracy how matter behaves, but they provide no explanation of why matter behaves in that way.*[3]

How are we to resolve this dichotomy? One approach attempts to remove it completely by postulating that consciousness is ubiquitous and inherent in everything. This theory is called *panpsychism* and was a staple of early Greek philosophers;[4] but it is enjoying a revival today in the form of the Integrated Information Theory of consciousness, first proposed by neuroscientist Giulio Tononi in 2004, which postulates that even simple systems, right down to subatomic particles, can possess some form of – albeit extremely rudimentary - consciousness. Modern panspyschism adherents claim that *all* matter has some associated mind or consciousness, and vice versa. Where there is mind there is matter, and where there is matter there is mind. These ideas are still hotly debated in the scientific community, and until mainstream science develops an integrated picture that includes the influence of consciousness in determining objective reality, by and large we are left to produce our own answers to this most equivocal question. Naturally, we can use our dowsing to gain answers to these mysteries, but we must always remember that the answers that we obtain are of necessity filtered through our own perceptions and world view, and are therefore prone to misinterpretation and unconscious bias. To paraphrase the late physicist Richard Feynman, the easiest person to fool is yourself'.[5]

Frankly, practically every form of dowsing today has become so infested with New Age pseudo-scientific thinking and downright 'woo-woo' that it is difficult to find a partisan platform on which to stand without facing ridicule from an ever-more vociferous pseudo-sceptical community, who are always quick to bring up the James Randi Million Dollar Challenge, as though it was the *de facto* proof of scientific validity. It is not, and anyway the challenge was withdrawn in 2015 - a fact rather conveniently overlooked by many sceptics more interested in bolstering their own feelings of superiority and pathological disbelief in anything that falls outside of their restricted world view.

Most likely, the majority of dowsers will be grouped somewhere along the curve between the two extremities of the spectrum, and we each adapt our personal dowsing model to accommodate our own particular belief system and experiences whilst remaining respectful of other's opinions. It doesn't mean that any one model is more 'correct' than another or that there is a 'right' or 'wrong' way to do things. It's more a matter of finding techniques and models that work for you and developing your own system. It is enough to know that dowsing works for you personally. We can leave the explanations of *how* it works to be discovered by those of a more theoretical and philosophical bent.

Having said that, I do think that it is important to apply scientific methodology to your dowsing whenever possible (always remembering that science is a *method* of doing things, not a doctrine). Using the scientific method, we first formulate a *question*, for example, "Why did my rods cross at that point?" Next, we develop a *hypothesis* – "Is that a water pipe?" Then, *prediction* – "If that was a water pipe, then this over *here* should be the same". The final two stages are *testing* – "Does that water pipe lead to this tap?" and *analysis* – "Can I find water pipes consistently using this method?"

Obviously, there are some situations, particularly when dowsing for intangible targets, when it may be difficult to fully verify our results, but nonetheless we always need to be questioning our findings and testing our results for consistency, and one of the most useful tools for the dowser is an air of healthy scepticism. If you find something that you can't explain or a result that doesn't make sense, ask yourself why that should be and design a sequence of further experiments to try to explain the situation, checking each step as you go. It is far too easy to be led astray by a chain of faulty reasoning in an attempt to justify an unexpected dowsing finding, and many dowsers, buoyed up by their own ego, fall into this trap of confirmatory bias.

This gives rise to the numerous dowsing superstitions or 'shibboleths' that are frequently passed on as perceived wisdom, such as that it is impossible to dowse accurately wearing Wellington boots, or that your dowsing reactions reverse with the phase of the moon. Or that dowsing over clay affects your depthing results, that your pendulum or rods need to be energetically cleansed regularly, and so on. For some dowsers, these beliefs may ultimately prove true because that's what they have been taught or have read somewhere; yet others have no trouble operating in identical circumstances. Everyone's methods are unique to them, and this is why it's difficult to get objective results about *anything* from different dowsers.

We each develop our own systems of measurement and classification from our experiences as we progress in our dowsing. As long as you are aware of that fact, and don't try to expound your particular dowsing system as universal truth, it needn't be an issue. It only becomes problematic when you try to explain your methods to non-dowsers, or share findings and techniques when working with other dowsers. In such circumstances, there is of necessity a period of adjustment and attuning to others' technique. This is referred to as 'calibration' and can easily be achieved by asking everyone to dowse for the same thing and comparing respective reactions – for instance, "How wide do you find this water vein to be?" Repeated dowsing of the same thing will result in everyone's reaction adjusting until a common mean is reached. Although this can seem confusing to the novice dowser, it's an especially useful technique to apply when a large group of dowsers are working on the same site simultaneously.

Similar reasoning can be applied to membership of a dowsing group (or any group for that matter) where it's difficult to maintain a common vocabulary unless the group regularly dowses together on the same projects. The Earth Energies Group (EEG) of the British Society of Dowsers was originally created with exactly this purpose in mind, at a time when dowsing for earth energies was a minefield of conflicting ideas. The EEG attempted to create just such a common vocabulary whereby Billy Gawn compiled the *Encyclopaedia of Terms*, which was discussed in Book One, and a new online edition of this glossary, together with the complete archive of EEG newsletters, is now available at britishdowsing.net.

Dowsing and Divination

Is dowsing the same as divination? Yes, at least when referring to the original sense of divination before it became inextricably entwined with fortune-telling and Ouija boards. As a verb, 'divine' is commonly used in relation to the act of water dowsing, as anyone who has seen the 2015 movie *The Water Diviner* featuring Russell Crowe can attest. But to divine also means, 'to discover something by guesswork *or intuition*' (emphasis added), and dowsing is, if you will, an *amplifier* of intuition. An experienced dowser learns to place great trust in the findings of their pendulum-enhanced intuition, eventually to the point where they often don't need to dowse the question; they will simply *know* the answer.

Dowsing invokes the Higher mind - the intuitive, creative, non-rational part of our consciousness, a source rarely available to the analytical Lower mind of everyday rational thought. It is the Higher mind that provides the source of our inspiration, our creativity, the unexplained flashes of insight that lead us to new discoveries and understandings. But this does not answer the question about the 'dowsing source' – is it purely the product of our Higher mind, or is there some external source involved?

Perhaps a better understanding can be gained if we stop thinking in terms of one singular source and take a look at the wider mechanisms governing divinatory systems in general. Occultist Ivo Dominguez Jr provides an interesting model in his book *Casting Sacred Space*, which I have adapted here into a format more suitable for our purposes. Consider the following diagram (Fig. 1) illustrating the three primary sources of divinatory information:

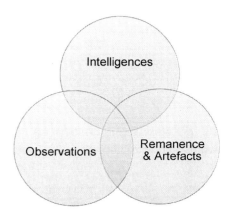

Figure 1: Sources of information

- Intelligences – Refers to information received from conscious sources, either our own individual consciousness, a collective group consciousness, or some external non-physical consciousness on any level of being.
- Remanence & Artefacts – Thoughts and actions leave an energetic imprint, or remanence, on places or objects, both physical and non-physical. This remanence is held in the information field and can be accessed remotely.

- Observations – We can draw upon our own empirical observations of events and situations and create meaning and pattern from them.

Arguably, our 'dowsing source' can be considered as a combination of all three modes. We can't classify it purely as an external intelligence, because our subconscious may be integrating data from the other two source areas to create a composite picture. For example, if we are dowsing for information relating to a tangible target, it's possible that we may be picking up a specific dowsing reaction from the target at the same time through the 'virtual bridge' of our dowsing tool. Likewise, if we have any prior empirical knowledge of the subject, our logical 'monkey brain' may subconsciously influence our interpretation of the result.

However it's received, the information is not always clear cut, as our internal psychic censor can obfuscate the truth. We may have too much attachment, either to our own belief systems or the subject of our questioning, causing us to be afraid of what we might find or misunderstand the information received. We may not have sufficient knowledge or vocabulary to know what it is that we are looking at, so the information may be lacking in detail.

Dowsing is just one method of divination and, because of the intermediary interface between questioner and source that the dowsing tool provides, circumvents many of the pitfalls presented by other means. By keeping our attention focused on the dowsing tool, we maintain a conscious connection with the outside world, keeping our metaphysical feet firmly planted on the ground.

Consider the following diagram (Fig. 2):

Figure 2: Modes of divination

- Tools & Systems – These refer to any divinatory system involving material tools, for instance Tarot, runes, *I Ching*, astrology, dowsing etc. Such systems can provide a safe, ordered structure for working by virtue of having an intermediary layer between source and questioner. Yet these same constructs can also lead to omissions or distortions if they are unable to accurately translate the information received.

- Psychic methods – Methods including clairvoyance, clairaudience, channelling, and similar means allow immediate direct access to the source. However, distortion can result since information must, of necessity, be filtered through the ego of the practitioner. There can also be safety issues with this type of working if there are no intermediary barriers between the source and receiver.

- Magick & Ritual – Information is gained through ceremonial access to intelligences and forces external to the practitioner. Although the structure of the ritual maintains a *status quo* and allows repeated attempts, it has the same issues of safety and veracity as the direct psychic approach.[6]

Most methods of divination involve something of all three approaches – even dowsing, although it is more firmly grounded in the 'tools and systems' category. Dowsing offers notable advantage over more traditional divination methods as it allows us access to areas of consciousness that are otherwise unavailable to us outside of trance states induced by hypnosis, meditation, ceremony and ritual or shamanic techniques, minus the inherent risks of direct psychic access or ceremonial practice. Just by having a pendulum in our hand and the ability to parse a series of relevant questions, we can seek information and get viable answers from these realms and their denizens without all the attendant ritual paraphernalia and extensive self-preparation techniques employed by more esoteric practitioners. The dowser does not need to spend hours memorising complex chants or ritual instructions, does not need an expensive collection of props and costume items to prepare themselves, nor do they need to perform complicated incantations or prolonged meditations to access this inner knowledge. With a bit of mental preparation to get into the 'dowsing zone' and competence in using a pendulum, the dowser can connect with and obtain information from any realm of experience; even causing change to occur in the real world through the use of dowsing and applied intent. They can affect and imprint energy patterns into substances or places that, in turn, can affect the way other humans react to them.

Through our dowsing, we are connecting to that fuzzy quantum realm of probabilities and, in effect, 'collapsing the wave function' into the pattern that we want to achieve. At this level, the advanced dowser is performing work that is to all intents and purposes indistinguishable from magick. The infamous adept Aleister Crowley defined magick as 'The Science and Art of causing Change to occur in conformity with Will'.[7] We can apply the same definition to advanced dowsing, where the dowser is not merely detecting but also applying intention to cause change. The central aim of any magickal operation is to bring about a reality change in accordance with the will of the operative. This involves quieting the conscious mind whilst holding a clear and focused intention to the exclusion of anything else, and dowsers happen to be particularly good at this. For us, the robes, incense, elaborate and lengthy ceremonies of traditional magick are mere window dressing. I would argue that, if you can clearly formulate your intention, visualise your desired result, and maintain your concentration in the 'dowsing zone' then, by any reasonable definition, you are doing magick. In that sense, we can say that dowsing is the new magick - the magick of the 21st Century.

Chapter 2

The Resonance of Water

> *We human beings consider ourselves to be made up of 'solid matter'. Actually, the physical body is the end product, so to speak, of the subtle information fields, which mould our physical body as well as all physical matter. These fields are holograms which change in time (and are) outside the reach of our normal senses. This is what clairvoyants perceive as colourful egg-shaped haloes or auras surrounding out physical bodies.*
>
> *- ITZHAK BENTOV, Stalking the Wild Pendulum*

All dowsers know that we are creatures of frequency, floating in a universe of frequencies. For centuries, occultists and mystics have spoken about feeling 'vibrations', and thanks to the flower children of the 1960s and '70s we now quite happily talk about feeling the 'vibes' of a place or event - well, those of us of a certain age group do! But have you ever considered what that actually means?

Einstein taught us that matter and energy are one and the same. What we perceive as matter is actually mostly empty space inhabited by tiny knots of vibrating energy. A common analogy compares the nucleus of an atom to a fly sitting in the centre of a sports stadium, with the stands representing the quantum fields of potentiality where the electrons may be found.

That's a whole lot of empty space. The nucleus itself, it turns out, is also mostly empty space, as we drill down deeper and deeper into protons, neutrons, quarks, and other subatomic particles. Within this sub-quantum world, we find the vibrating knots of energy described in String Theory, in which the familiar point-like solid particles of particle physics are replaced by one-dimensional vibrating objects called *strings*. At larger scales, a string looks just like an ordinary particle, with its mass, charge, and other properties determined by the vibrational state of the string. String theory is still a bit of a work in progress and hasn't yet completely overwritten the 'standard model' of particle physics, yet it offers some interesting ideas that may help reconcile the differences between general relativity and quantum mechanics.

Key features of string theory include the concept that all objects in our Universe are composed of vibrating filaments (*strings*), and membranes ('*branes*) of energy; that additional dimensions to the Universe *must* exist; that there may be parallel universes to our own, and that our Universe may exhibit holographic principles. This last idea dates to earlier works by physicists David Bohm and Karl Pribram, perhaps best explored for the general reader in Michael Talbot's 1991 book *The Holographic Universe*. More recently, a mathematical proof of the concept has been proposed by scientists at the University of Southampton working in conjunction with colleagues in Canada and Italy. They suggest that, just as our perception of a 3D movie as having length, breadth and depth comes from a flat 2D surface, so our perception of reality and time arises from mathematics encoded as a 2D boundary enclosing the entire cosmos. Although this idea is nigh-impossible to envisage even for the scientists who came up with it, the maths behind it checks out and provides a link between Einstein's theory of gravity and quantum theory.[1]

We might also consider the *anthropic principle*, which states that the mere fact that humanity exists can be an explanation for certain physical properties of our Universe. In order for the Universe to be observable in the first place, it must be compatible with the conscious and sentient life that observes it.[2] This idea is really a logical consequence of the famous double-slit experiment in quantum mechanics, which unequivocally demonstrates that fundamental particles like electrons can display characteristics of both waves and particles at the same time, and that the outcome of the experiment is determined by the act of observation by the experimenter - we looked at this in Book 1, but I'll recap it here for new readers.

Imagine throwing a whole lot of tennis balls coated with paint at a wall with two vertical slits in it, with a second wall behind. Most of the balls will bounce off the first wall, but some will go through the slits and leave paint marks on the second wall which will, when enough balls have hit it, show two stripe marks roughly corresponding to the vertical slits. Now, imagine that instead of tennis balls, we shine light of a single wavelength (such as a laser beam) through the slits. If the distance between the slits is roughly the same as the light's wavelength, the slits act as two new sources, with the light waves spreading out like ripples from two stones thrown into water. The peaks and troughs of each wave interfere with each other, and instead of the two vertical patterns on the back wall, we now see a series of alternating light and dark bands extending outwards - an interference pattern.

Strangeness arises when we go quantum and start firing particles like electrons at the two slits. Here, as the particles are tiny pieces of matter, you would expect to get two vertical stripes like the tennis balls. Instead, what we see is an interference pattern. Even when single electrons are fired at the slits one at a time, they produce an interference pattern on the rear wall after the experiment is left to run for a while. It is as though the single electron somehow splits in two, passing through both slits simultaneously before recombining to hit the rear wall as part of an interference pattern - completely baffling behaviour. To try and understand what is happening here, physicists placed a detector by the slits, to record (or 'observe') which one the electron actually passed through. But when they did so, the electrons stopped behaving like a wave and acted like well-behaved little particles once more, producing two vertical stripes. It's as if the electrons *know* that they're being watched and decide to behave like good little tennis balls.[3]

If this experiment is to be believed (and it has been replicated several times), then particles in the quantum realm somehow manage to combine characteristics of both particles and waves at the same time. This is called the *wave-particle duality* in quantum mechanics. It suggests that reality is somewhat fuzzy, that things exist first as a field of probabilities until the act of conscious observation 'collapses the wave function' and determines how they will manifest. Or to put it another way, *we create the reality we desire.* Extrapolating this idea back to the creation of our Universe, you could argue that physicists actually created the Universe the way it is, simply by the act of observing the Big Bang. Perhaps we are indeed our own gods? But possibly that particular philosophical line of reasoning is better debated over a couple of beers in the pub of an evening. For the purpose of this book, let's just take on board the concept that all objects in our Universe, including ourselves, are composed of vibrating knots of energy. We are truly Beings of frequency and vibration, and it's in this sea of potential that the dowser works.

Water and Consciousness

It's generally believed that American dowser Leslie L Mooney first discovered, back in the early 1960s, that it's possible to influence the presence and quality of water within a borehole. Where a borehole is fed by two or more water veins and one of them had become polluted, had a high sulphur content or some other impurity that affected the potability of the water, Leslie found that it was possible to divert the polluted vein by inserting a metal crowbar into the ground next to the vein and hammering it with a mallet in the direction he wanted the vein to move.[4] This same method was (and still is) used to divert water veins away from basements and cellars where seepage is a problem. I've had some experience of this myself.

An architect who was constructing a new sunken extension for a client's property called me in to track down an annoying water seepage problem. The irony of the situation was that the extension housed a swimming pool! The extension was set into sloping ground, and although the troublesome water was not penetrating the clay surround of the pool itself (which had not been filled), it was running down the side underneath a stepped tile walkway and collecting at the lower end, where it eventually penetrated through the floor tiles. The leakage became so severe that it required the installation of a pump running 24/7 to keep things from flooding. In order to trace the source of this water, I first of all dowsed over the water in the sump to try and gauge the 'flavour' of the water. For this, I used a Mager Rosette (see Book 1) and asked if there was a unique colour combination that I could use to identify this particular water. The Mager Rosette reacted to two colours in response to this (the first time it had done so and the first time I had tried this method). After some experimentation using an alternative source of water from the tap to establish a 'control', I was confident that this was indeed a unique code in this situation that would allow me to identify water from the same source as that collecting in the sump.

Suitably primed with this information, I proceeded to dowse around the garden outside the extension, which was not easy because of its proximity to the boundary wall on one side that boasted a proliferation of dense and pointy foliage. However, I eventually dowsed two water veins, either of which could have been responsible for the leakage, and I soon identified the correct one using my colour combination technique. The other vein did not react to either of the two colours that I was looking for, but just to be certain I used my pendulum to ascertain the depths of both veins. The second vein (the one that didn't react to my colour code) was too deep to be responsible for the leakage, but the first one dowsed at around two and a half metres in depth, which was exactly right to be the offending leak.

Having explained my findings and told him that I was going to attempt to divert the vein away from the extension, I then of course had to explain the theory behind this procedure to an increasingly sceptical-looking architect. To his credit, he agreed to let me try it and left me to get on with things. Selecting the largest steel rod I had with me (45cm of 15mm diameter steel), I tuned in and dowsed the best spot to insert the rod to manifest the desired diversion of the stream. Then, after dowsing how far to insert the rod and how many times I would need to hit it to achieve the required diversion, all the while picturing in my head the direction that I wanted the water to move, I hammered the rod into the ground for about half its length and then hit the side of the rod the designated number of times in the direction I wanted to move the water. Dowsing suggested that it would take a couple of days for the vein to completely clear the extension, but after 20 minutes or so I dowsed the position of the vein and it clearly appeared to be moving to where I wanted it to go. I demonstrated this to the architect and asked him to, "Give it a day or two" to see how things went.

I was slightly disappointed to learn that, although my 'fix' appeared to be working, the architect decided the very next day that it was safer to adopt a 'belt and braces' approach by digging a separate drainage trench across the offending water vein to permanently remove the problem before it reached the extension. Still, I can't really blame him as I suppose he had more to lose financially than I did. At least I was able to correctly identify the offending stream for him.

This technique of diverting water veins has been successfully used by several dowsers, and of course it didn't take long for the reverse hypothesis to be put into effect – if a well had run dry or the flow needed to be increased and there was a convenient vein nearby, exactly the same method can be used to divert the vein into the dry well or borehole. Mooney thought that it was based on a purely mechanical principle of harmonic sound waves propagating through the earth and causing the water to follow the path of least resistance, but clearly intention plays a significant role in the technique, as later dowsers have demonstrated.

Veteran American water dowser John Wayne Blassingame, who has over 40 years' experience and claims a better than 95% success rate, developed an interesting device to help with the control of water veins. He manufactured an offset T-bar (Fig. 3) that he calls an 'amplifier'. It bears a passing resemblance to a water stopcock key, but the top horizontal bar is offset so that the junction with the upright is set at the Golden Proportion division of the horizontal bar. The length of the upright is also in Golden Proportion to the length of the crossbar. After hammering it into the ground, but before hammering on the side of the device to divert the water, John will align it so that the longer part of the crossbar is pointing in the direction he wants the vein to move.

John also uses his T-bar to save time when locating water on large properties. He will hammer the rod into the ground at the edge of the area, then slowly rotate the top bar while dowsing with his L-rod in his free hand, asking for a reaction when the arm of the T-bar is pointing towards the water

Figure 3: John Wayne Blassingame (with Susan Collins) and his T-bar (photo: Susan Collins)

source that he is looking for. He then repeats this procedure from a second, and then a third, position to triangulate the final location. John also sometimes uses the device as a remote dowsing tool to save him having to do a lot of walking. Once he has inserted the T-rod and rotated it to ascertain the direction to walk to find the best water according to his dowsing parameters, John asks the landowner to take some marker flags and walk in the direction that the T-rod is pointing until John's L-rod gives the desired reaction, whereupon he will yell at them to stop and put in a marker flag. In effect, the landowner is acting as a remote sensor. After repeating this procedure another couple of times to get the triangulation, they will have marked out a relatively small area which John can then dowse - or ask the client to dowse - to pinpoint the final location for the drill.[5]

It is interesting to compare this method of hammering metal stakes into the ground with the standard 'fix' adopted by many dowsers in cases of geopathic stress, where a steel rod is hammered into the water vein carrying the stress, which seems to neutralise or dissipate the detrimental energy from that point onwards. This 'earth acupuncture' method was developed by Bruce MacManaway who found his own healing gift on the beaches of Normandy during the Second World War when he had run out of most medical supplies and resorted to direct hands-on healing. After the war, Bruce was instrumental in developing the modern spiritual healing network in Britain that we have today, and introduced his method for removing geopathic stress using the earth acupuncture technique to many dowsers, both in Britain and abroad, in particular the renowned American dowser Terry Ross, who was one of the founder members of the American Society of Dowsers. Terry spread the technique widely in North America through his teachings and writings.

At some stage, more advanced dowsers like former American Society of Dowsers (ASD) Presidents Dwin Gordon and Terry Ross discovered that it wasn't necessary to actually hammer a crowbar into the ground to divert the water, or even to be present on-site at all. Distance is not a factor for the proficient dowser and, just as it is possible to dowse remotely on a map, they found that they could manipulate water veins in this way purely through the application of focused intention at a distance. Terry Ross records several examples of this in his book *The Divining Mind*.[6] Clearly this offers great advantage to the dowser, as it becomes possible to fix many related problems for clients who are many miles away, even on the other side of the world, without the need to visit the property. Dwin Gordon is even on record as having remotely 'called in' extra water to farms where the existing borehole supply had become insufficient to meet the needs of an expanding dairy herd and where he could not detect sufficient water elsewhere on the property to justify drilling an additional borehole. On these occasions, when his dowsing suggested that the new water was coming from a source much deeper than the original supply and would take a couple of days to reach the borehole, the enhanced supply would duly appear right on schedule, even to the hour.[7]

A tale from northern Vermont recounts how local dowser Edith Greene saved the town of Montgomery from a major water crisis back in 2004 when dangerous quantities of arsenic were discovered in the town's inadequate reservoir. Despite paying out thousands of dollars for hydrogeologists to drill several boreholes, they had not managed to find an adequate supply to replace the reservoir, until an enlightened female councillor decided to ask Edith to dowse at a site that had been rejected by the scientists.

Edith spent the best part of a cold winter's day dowsing the area, leaving markers at promising positions, but by the end of the day she had not definitively pinpointed the best site. When she returned the next day, she was surprised (and rather upset) to see the drilling operation already well underway using one of her temporary markers as a guide. Fortunately, they did find a plentiful source of water - three times more than needed for the town supply - but when a sample was sent for analysis, the lab told them that it contained elevated levels of uranium, which naturally occurred in the bedrock of the area. At the town meeting, Edith announced that this wasn't a problem as she could purify the water using intent to remove the uranium, but this claim was met with scepticism and even muffled laughter from the councillors. Nevertheless, she was told to 'go for it', and went off to do her thing. She had experience of removing radon gas from people's basements and didn't see why removing uranium from water should be any different.

There is more to this story, but the upshot is that by early 2005 the uranium had all but vanished from the water, to everyone's amazement. Yet the councillors simply could not believe that it had been the result of Edith's dowsing, and they consequently reneged on payment of her $400 fee. It was okay for them to accept that a dowser can somehow find underground water, but to actively remove uranium from it...? Well, that was too much like witchcraft for their scientific mind-sets.[8]

There are clear parallels between these remote dowsing interventions and distant healing, and the connections between water dowsing and healing are pretty strong; perhaps not surprising given that the human body has over 60% water content. Which leads us to the concept that water has a 'memory' and can store intention, the very foundation of homeopathy.

In 1988, French biologist Jacques Beneviste published a controversial article in the prestigious scientific journal *Nature*, describing an experiment where heavily-diluted and violently-agitated solutions of antibodies had an effect on human basophil cells identical to that caused by the original antibody - an allergic reaction in effect - even though no molecules of antibody could conceivably be present in the diluted solution. This seemed to validate the homeopathic method of extreme dilution and sucussion to create remedies, although it defied any known scientific explanation. Although Beneviste's study was seen by homoeopathists as clear vindication of its efficacy, the study caused huge ructions in the scientific community, and *Nature* editor John Maddox insisted that the experiments should be re-run under the supervision of a hand-picked group of observers. These included himself, chemist and freelance debunker Walter Stewart, and none other than stage conjuror and arch-sceptic James Randi, who proffered his usual 'million-dollar challenge', which seems to have become the sceptics' preferred gold standard of scientific legitimacy. The experiments were repeated under various control conditions but were by and large unsuccessful except for those where the technician was aware of which test tube contained the active sample, or where the experimenter was sympathetic to the outcome. Or to look at it another way, where the *consciousness* of the technician was involved in creating the diluted sample. To the sceptical observers, this was unmistakable evidence of experimenter bias, and the whole project was dismissed, although the controversy raged in the letters page of *Nature* and elsewhere for many years. Beneviste compared the sceptical scrutiny he endured to "McCarthy-like persecution or Salem witch-hunts", even accusing Randi of hoodwinking the experimenters by distracting them with magic tricks.[9]

Beneviste found one sympathetic scientist in the form of Nobel laureate Brian Josephson, with whom continued working, culminating in a series of papers between 1997 and 2000 which claimed that the effect could be recorded electromagnetically, then digitised and transmitted electronically, even over the internet, where the electronic 'signature' could be subsequently applied to a container of water, converting it to a homeopathic remedy. An independent test carried out in 2000 by an American team funded by the US Department of Defense failed to find any effect except when one of Beneviste's original team was running the equipment. Beneviste commented that he had noticed this himself, and that certain individuals consistently obtained results where others got no effects. Here again, we can either ascribe this to experimenter bias, downright fraud, or the effect of positive *intent* on the outcome of the experiment. This 'belief' effect has been scientifically demonstrated in various tests over the years. Several examples - where experimental results have been dramatically enhanced when the participants believed in the effect they were trying to emulate - are discussed by American parapsychologist Dean Radin in his excellent 2018 book, *Real Magic.*[10]

Although this sort of effect falls outside of the scientific paradigm, it is well-established in popular consciousness. Catholics happily accept that holy water blessed by the intent of a priest has healing and protective powers, and water as an activating agent plays a part in many folk rituals around the world to invoke divine aid or grant an individual's wish. Often such rituals involve anointing a stone with water (or sometimes milk), as though the stone contains some sort of animistic spirit that is nourished by the liquid bestowments. Offertory stones are called *Bullauns* in Ireland and *Dobby Stanes* in Scotland.[11] This is an interesting area of study in itself, and I offer a few examples of such *petromancy* for consideration.

The dolmen of Rocenaud in France has prehistoric cup-marks, some groupings of which suggest the constellation of the Pleiades. Local tradition suggests that knocking in the cup-marks with a flint can cause the wind to change. An account by Frances M. Gostling, in her 1909 book *Bretons at Home*, details how a rainy south-westerly wind was invoked for her benefit using this technique.[12]

At the *Fontaine de Barenton* (Fig. 4), a legendary holy spring deep in the *Forêt de Paimpont* in Brittany, where the water visibly bubbles out of the ground, the local populace and priest would process through the forest in times of drought to invoke the magical powers of the spring by ceremonially dousing the capstone (a recycled *menhir* - now broken and mostly missing) with the sacred waters. According to local

Figure 4: Fontaine de Barenton

tradition, this never fails to evoke a thunderstorm. The last recorded instance of this ritual taking place was in 1921, when it successfully produced rain, and anecdotal accounts suggest that the ritual is still performed today.

The Clachnacuddin stone (Fig. 5), now ensconced in the

plinth of the mercat cross outside Inverness town hall, once marked the spot where local women would rest their baskets of laundry on their way to and from the riverside (*Clachnacuddin* means 'stone of the tubs'). Water splashed onto the stone was thought to ensure good fortune, and presumably a clean wash! The stone was moved to its present position and set into the plinth to prevent emigrant Invernesians from chipping a piece off to protect them when away from

Figure 5: Inverness Clachnacuddin Stone and mercat cross

their home; but it is still said that the fortunes of the town itself depend on the stone remaining in place, and in 2011 the careless dumping of some metal barriers on the stone by workmen resulted in a flurry of outrage in the letters page of the local paper.

The Heart of Midlothian (Fig. 6) is a heart-shaped mosaic situated on Edinburgh's historic Royal Mile. It marks the entrance to the old Tolbooth, and popular tradition has it that you should spit into the centre of it as you pass by to bring good

Figure 6: Heart of Midlothian

fortune. However, there is a more macabre interpretation of this custom, as the Tolbooth was the place where condemned prisoners were held before being taken out to be hanged on this spot. Spitting on the Heart was a way of showing contempt for the practice.

Another famous Scottish stone is the Stone of Mannan (Fig. 7), which is to be found in the main square of Clackmannan (the town is named after the stone), next to the old mercat cross and the Tolbooth. It is curious to see these three historical items vying for the prerogative of official town *omphalos.* The Mannan stone, a pre-Christian stone dedicated to the Celtic sea-god *Manannán mac Lir* (hence another connection with

Figure 7: Mannan stone (right)

water), is curiously perched out of reach on top of a 3.5m megalithic splinter of stone, where it was placed in the 19th Century, giving the entire edifice a distinctly phallic appearance. It is tempting to hypothesise that this was an act of civic control to prevent people throwing water or spitting on it to invoke the power of the stone, or to prevent them chipping pieces off it (as happened in Inverness). In recent years, the town Council proposed moving the stone so that they could remodel the traffic flow in the square, but this produced such an outcry from local people, claiming that it would bring disaster on the town, that the scheme was quickly abandoned.

A rather different ritual that utilises water to invoke the power of a stone involves a custom formerly practised by the children of Faifley on the western outskirts of Glasgow, where they would *urinate* into the prehistoric cup-and-ring markings on the Cochno Stone (Fig. 8) - widely regarded as the most significant rock art panel in Europe. Now, of course it's unlikely that they were doing this with any specific intent; but

Figure 8: The Cochno Stone

nonetheless it is arguably a residual folk-memory of community water rituals. A local resident told me that they also used to break open fireworks and fill the markings on the stone with the gunpowder which they then set alight - another example of using an elemental aid, in this case fire, to set your intent into a stone. These and other acts of vandalism led to the stone being buried in 1964 to prevent further damage. A full excavation was carried out in 2016 by Glasgow University Archaeology Department under the direction of Dr Kenny Brophy, to allow a full 3D LIDAR scan and photogrammetric survey to be conducted in conjunction with digital restoration specialists Factum Arte, with the stated aim of producing a full-size replica stone once sufficient funding can be raised. The stone was then re-buried.

This idea of stones possessing mystical powers (often of a healing nature) that are activated by water is an old one indeed. In the 18th Century, a local tradition surrounding Stonehenge recorded that scrapings from the stones of the monument, when washed with water, would heal any recent wound or old sore on the body. Geoffrey of Monmouth, in his semi-apocryphal *History of the Kings of Britain*, accords special healing powers to the 'washing stones' of the sacred Hill of Uisneach in Ireland. The stones in both cases were said to have been empowered by Merlin.[13]

Perhaps the most renowned recent demonstration of the effect of intention on water is shown by the experiments carried out by the late Dr Masuro Emoto, whose many photographs of frozen water crystals seem to dramatically demonstrate that water has a 'memory' and is affected, not only by any pollutants it carries, but also by human emotions and intention. Crystals generated using water from polluted lakes show a very distorted form, whereas crystals from water gathered at sacred springs, or water that had been blessed or prayed over, were more geometrically perfect.

Emoto's work has been replicated by other researchers. Worthy of mention here is Rasmus Gaupp-Berghausen, an agricultural scientist who runs Dr Emoto's Hado-Life Europe laboratory in Liechtenstein. Initially, Rasmus invited Dr Emoto to visit Europe with the intention of debunking his work; however, on discovering that he could replicate his results, became a convert and spent the next several years travelling and lecturing with Dr Emoto. I was fortunate enough to meet them both at a lecture in Glasgow, and subsequently invited Rasmus to present at the BSD's 2014 conference. Their laboratory has sampled over 2,000 water samples from all over the world, from holy springs like Lourdes and Fatima, healing wells and spas, to normal springs and tap water. One of the more interesting findings demonstrates that water seemingly has the property of reacting to any kind of vibration, be it ultrasound, microwaves, or simply music. Each has a particular effect on the way the water crystals form during freezing, and the more harmonic the vibration, the more this harmony is reflected in the formation of beautiful geometric shapes in the water as it freezes. Rasmus found that the easiest way to create these beautiful water crystals was to play harmonious music. Playing simple harmonic intervals like the octave and the major fifth resulted in quite distinct crystal forms, with the fifth producing exceptionally beautiful crystals. It is clear from these experiments that water is not just a passive liquid but a responsive fluid that reacts to stimuli.

Rasmus' work has since progressed to working with ultrasound and its effect on amniotic fluid. With the near-ubiquitous use of ultrasound in pre-natal examinations, this represents a major area of research; the main hypothesis of the work being that a more harmonic and structured ultrasound signal has a beneficial effect on the amniotic fluid and the foetus growing within.

A key finding of Rasmus' work of relevance to dowsers is that *too much* intention can disrupt the formation of the water crystals. When he first tried to create his own crystals in the laboratory to replicate Emoto's experiments, Rasmus struggled for several months without managing to create any viable crystals, whether attempting to program the intent himself, or using water samples sent to him from around the world where the sample had been prayed, meditated, chanted over or otherwise charged with intention. None of the samples would form proper crystals like those produced by Emoto's team. He was in despair and on the verge of telling Dr Emoto that he no longer wished to continue with this work, when suddenly the crystals started to appear. It was as if they were waiting for him to stop trying so hard. This, he says, is why the easiest way to make the crystals is by playing music, or taping words or symbols to the water container; it seems that continually applied intention actually militates against successful crystal formation, and it's only when the intention is *withdrawn* that crystals will form. Rasmus says, "It doesn't work because *intention* is a judgement – 'I want to change the water, I am willing this water to change'. The moment you *want* to make a crystal, it doesn't appear. What is needed is *attention*, not intention. The moment you simply *love*, the crystal appears."[14]

Although this conclusion might be startling to dowsers, it fits perfectly with the rationale behind spellcasting in the world of traditional witchcraft and magick. Here the practitioner spends a lot of time constructing and energising the spell through ceremony and ritual, all the while holding and focusing their intention; the spell is then 'released' at the climax of the ritual, and from that point on it *must be forgotten about* or it will likely fail. The magickal energy must be allowed to manifest in its own way without further interference. Much of the methodology of ceremonial magick is really about encoding the intention behind the spell in such a complicated and confusing manner that the analytical part of the practitioner's brain shuts off and lets the subconscious deal with the actual work – and of course this is exactly the same mental condition that dowsers strive to achieve. The magician will prepare by first cleansing himself, donning his robes and assembling his working tools. He will then set up his working space by drawing and casting a protective circle, followed by a period of meditation or prayer to clear his mind, before performing a complex series of rituals to purify and banish any negative influences from the circle, finally invoking a suitable god-form, spirit guide or other influence to aid in the working. Only then is he ready to craft his spell, evoke spirits, or do whatever he set out to achieve with the ritual. By this stage, he has inflamed himself by holding such a state of focused concentration for so long that the analytical part of the brain has all but shut down, leaving him in a profoundly altered state of consciousness and allowing a clear channel for the subconscious to come through. Once the spell has been completed at the climax of the ritual, the practitioner will close down the working space and do his best to forget about the working; this is essential to avoid interference. Often the practitioner is genuinely surprised when they get the desired result from the working (this is also partly why initiates are advised to keep a magickal diary, so that they can return and check on their work, later).

There is an aphorism popular amongst both witches and magicians that runs, "To Know, to Will, to Dare, to Keep Silent". It is known as the 'Witch's Pyramid', the 'Four Powers of the Sphinx' or the 'Four Cornerstones' in Hermetic magick. It is usually attributed to Eliphas Levi and refers to the manner in which the practitioner is supposed to conduct themself. Levi writes about it thus:

> *The great secret of magic, the unique and incommunicable Arcana, has for its purpose the placing of supernatural power at the service of the human will in some way.*
> *To attain such an achievement it is necessary to KNOW what has to be done, to WILL what is required, to DARE what must be attempted and to KEEP SILENT with discernment.* [15]

The same formula is applied to the casting of a spell – the practitioner needs to KNOW what the requirements of the ritual are, have the WILL to carry out the ritual and remain focused throughout, DARE to face any fears and uncertainties and carry it through to the end, and finally to KEEP SILENT afterwards until the results have manifested.

Seen in this light, Rasmus' statement regarding intention vs. attention makes a lot more sense, and as dowsers I think we can all learn something from this. From my own experience I would certainly agree that it is possible to jinx a dowsing 'fix' by thinking too hard and for too long about the result. There are some cases where it is better to do the work and leave something permanently in place to hold the intention so that the dowser can stop thinking about what the result *should* be and instead pay attention to what *is*. The 'something' can be a physical object (or objects) - even a simple drawing or written affirmation - or it can be an energetically programmed assertion executed using the dowsing tool. For a more in-depth explanation of this, see my companion book *Dowsing with Sigils - a Dowsing Magic Workbook.*

Chapter 3

Geopathic Stress

Geopathic stress is typically defined as prolonged, repeated exposure to damaging earth energies. Consequences include disease and dysfunction of a repeating or chronic nature, unresponsive to therapeutic intervention and typically showing up after a move to a new domestic or work location. Sleeping long and waking tired and other dysfunctions of biological rhythms is typical. Geopathic stress is most easily identified and assessed through dowsing, kinesiology or Vega analysis, and the energy fields causing it are related to various tangible and intangible elements in the earths structure, both physical and energetic.

-- DR PATRICK MACMANAWAY

Geopathic comes from two Greek words: *geo* meaning 'of the earth', and *pathos*, meaning 'suffering'. The word 'geopathic' literally means 'suffering of the Earth'. The term 'geopathic stress' generally refers to changes in the natural geomagnetic field of the earth caused by geological fault lines, mineral and crystal deposits, underground water flows, quarries, mine workings, caves, cavities, or other features. Dowsing allows us to detect the presence, and assess the nature and quality of, these disturbances, as well as other subtle earth energy flows possessing a nature analogous to the meridians of *chi* running in the human body that feature in traditional Chinese medicine and acupuncture. *Chi* paths have gone by many names in diverse cultures, including 'dragons', 'song lines', 'spirit paths', and 'ley lines'. Nowadays, we tend to include psycho-spiritual disturbances, and even man-made electromagnetic issues, under the same umbrella category of geopathic stress, although the term 'technopathic stress' is more common in the latter instance.

Depending on the strength and character of the earth energies present, a location may be a healthy and beneficial one for human presence and activity, it may be indifferent to human presence, or it may be potentially harmful and undermining to human health at physical, emotional, mental, or spiritual levels. Plants and animals have varying sensitivities to earth energies; some species thrive in locations that are healthy for humans, and other species thrive in areas considered detrimental for humans. There are, therefore, no 'good' or 'bad' energies, simply ones that humans can healthily relate to and others that may be more challenging.

In traditional cultures possessing strong awareness of these landscape energies, people know how to select appropriate landscapes with a high energetic level for places of spiritual working, and calmer and low-energy areas for domestic situations. They will avoid areas that are potentially damaging for human habitation or activity. Yet in contemporary societies, with growing populations leading to ever-increasing demands for new housing, constructing homes and workplaces in inappropriate areas where the energies are detrimental to human health is now commonplace, resulting in greatly increased incidence of geopathic stress.

Historical Overview

Geopathic stress is not new. It's been known about at least since the 1920s when German scientist-dowsers started documenting *'Krebshausen'* – houses with an unusually high incidence of cancer cases that they discovered were situated over geological fault lines. The first crucial study was by two German researchers Winzer & Melzer, who divided the city of Stuttgart into districts of varying cancer incidence, attempting to find correlation with distinct types of bedrock geology. Failing in this, and following advice from local dowsers, they instead looked at the five major geological fault lines traversing the city and found that these faults corresponded closely with the areas of highest cancer mortality. They proposed that some sort of telluric radiation, emanating from the fault lines, might be responsible for higher incidences of cancer.[1]

In *Dowsing Magic - Book 1*, we looked at other historical research into geopathic stress, in particular Baron von Pohl's 1929 work in the Bavarian town of Vilsbiburg and Pierre Cody's research in the 1930s. Cody's work defined the width and height of stress lines, using electroscopes to check the concentration of airborne ions over water. By recording the distance from the vein at which the electroscope discharged, he demonstrated that the geopathic radiation rose vertically in a tight band above the water, even passing through several floors of a multi-storey building. Lead sheets placed under the electroscopes prevented them from discharging and, over the course of a week or so, developed discolouration in the area directly over the water vein, leading Cody to conclude that there must be a weakly radioactive component to the radiation. This was later confirmed by researchers Josef Wüst in 1955, who detected small increases in gamma radiation in geopathic zones, and Jakob Stängle in the 1970s, who developed an extremely sensitive scintillation counter designed to measure weak gamma radiation and other charged particles. After conclusively replicating von Pohl's survey of Vilsbiburg, Stängle concluded:

> *The principal objection against the existence of pathogenic stimulation zones, namely the inability to objectify them, is no longer valid.*

More recently, Swiss nuclear physicist Angelo Communetti repeated Cody's experiments with electroscopes in high-rise buildings and found that the column of radiation deviated 15 degrees eastwards from the vertical in tall buildings, suggesting some correspondence with the rotation of the Earth.[2]

Animal and plant studies

It's not only humans who are affected by geopathic zones. Many dairy farmers and horse breeders will be familiar with the phenomenon of an empty stall in their barn or stable where animals housed there for extended periods of time become ill. In the 1970s Dr Joseph Kopp, a consulting geologist and dowser in Switzerland made a breakthrough discovery when he was dowsing a water vein in Grabs, in the Sankt Gallen canton. He noted that the vein ran directly under a new barn, which was empty. On inquiry, he found that so many of the animals had fallen ill in the barn that the owner had abandoned it. This led Kopp to undertake a survey of 130 barns in which animals confined for prolonged periods of time had developed illnesses running from severe rheumatism of the joints to repeated miscarriages, sickly calves, uterine deterioration, and reduced milk yield in the case of dairy cows. He noted the presence of underground water veins in every barn studied. When the animals were moved out of the affected stalls, they eventually recovered; conversely, healthy animals placed into the stalls quickly became sick. I have encountered several such 'sick stalls' on farms during dowsing consultations and, in every case, found geopathic underground water affecting the stall in question. It's less of a problem on contemporary dairy farms as the animals are usually given free rein of the barn and don't have assigned stalls, so they are not spending prolonged periods in the geopathic zones. But horse stables, where the animals usually *do* have their own individual stalls, can still exhibit these problems. The geopathic stress can also cause uncharacteristic behavioural changes in the animals affected, and such anomalies often disappear when the animal is re-housed.

In her doctoral thesis, Polish agricultural scientist Dr Barbara Tombarkiewicz researched how changes in the geomagnetic field affect animals. Her thesis studied the health of 309 cows kept in separate stalls in a building measuring 91 x 24 metres in area. The farmer reported that cows kept in three particular stalls always suffered ill health. Initially, the problem was resolved by moving these unhealthy cows to other stalls in the complex, where they recovered. However, healthy cows placed in the three affected stalls soon began to exhibit similar health problems. Magnetometer readings recorded in the problematic stalls showed pronounced variations in the local geomagnetic field strength. The three stalls were found to be located over magnetic anomalies of 34,000nT (nanotesla) / 340mG (milligauss). Blood analysis of the animals in the affected stalls revealed lower counts of essential trace elements such as aluminium, zinc, copper, and iron, as well as low leukocyte (white blood cells) counts. Dr Tombarkiewicz's report concluded that the microelement disorders in the animals housed in the geopathic stalls was the primary cause of the many ailments.

The influence of geopathic stress on a living organism is slow and cumulative over time, eventually leading to dysfunction and disease that can, in many cases, be reversed once the organism is removed from the disturbance zone, as Dr Tombarkiewicz's research demonstrates. Plants can also be affected by geopathic zones, displaying poor leaf growth and low fruit yields. Potatoes and root vegetables stored in cellars will rot faster if stored in a cellar where there is geopathic stress. Frequently, a line of geopathic stress can be traced visually across a property by looking for gaps in hedges, poor plant growth, dead and distorted trees and so on. I have noticed this in several properties where I have dowsed the interior before discovering a tell-tale gap in the hedge where the stress line crosses.

Austrian dowser Käthe Bachler also researched plant and tree growth and found that some fruiting trees such as apple and pear were most affected by geopathic areas, as were nut, beech and lime/linden trees, lilacs, and sunflowers. Conversely, other fruiting trees such as cherry, plum, nectarine, peach and elderberry trees appear to function *better* on geopathic lines, as do mistletoe-bearing trees. Oak and fir trees have an affinity for stress-bearing underground water veins and should be avoided in thunderstorms as they have a tendency to attract lightning; something that is recorded in the folklore rhyme, *"Beware the oak; it draws the stroke".*

Bachler also reported that dogs, horses, cows, pigs, chickens, and birds will naturally avoid these geopathic zones, whereas cats, bees, ants, insects, and bacteria will thrive on the same energies. Most dowsers know that cats seem to be attracted to geopathic areas and a cat's regular sleeping spot, in the absence of other indicators like underfloor heating pipes, sunbeams, or other warm areas, can be a good indicator of the presence of a geopathic line. Dogs, on the other hand, seem to have similar sensibilities to humans where geopathic stress is concerned.

I have encountered this a few times, but the most dramatic example involved a client where I noticed that the dog basket, placed in front of a French window, did not appear to have been slept in. When I asked about this, I was told that they had moved the basket there only a few weeks previously, but the dog did not like sleeping in it and preferred the sofa. Of course, this particular window was exactly where I had previously dowsed the geopathic line entering the property and was located directly underneath the main bedroom on the upper floor.

Bachler is, however, better known for her research on humans, documented in her best-selling 1976 book *Earth Radiation*,[3] which contains results gathered from dowsing some 3,000 cases in 14 countries and interviews with 11,000 people. Her extensive investigations led her to conclude that 95% of chronically and severely ill people have their sleeping or working places directly above noxious water veins. She also checked around 500 cases of cancer and found that every person was sleeping over underground water. Her discovery that the desks of unruly and poorly-performing schoolchildren were always situated in a geopathic zone led her to recommend the concept of 'rolling classrooms', where classes would change their seating arrangements every 2-3 weeks so that no one was spending too long over the area in question. Many schools in Austria and elsewhere adopted this technique following her recommendations.

Bachler was also an early exponent of building biology and wrote about the dangers of electromagnetic fields (EMFs), warning against having electrical appliances near the bed or against adjacent walls and recommending wooden-framed beds and natural fibre mattresses. This 'technopathic stress', or electrical hyper-sensitivity, has become more of a focus in recent years with the proliferation of wireless communications technologies. Growing numbers of people are becoming sensitive to these radiations, in some cases to the extent that they have to live apart from society in isolated areas where there are fewer microwave emissions from phone towers and public Wi-Fi networks. The valley around the Green Bank radio telescope in West Virginia, a designated National Radio Quiet Zone, has become a haven for sufferers because of its strict controls on radio emissions. Nokia's former Chief Technology Officer, Matti Niemelä, even blames exposure to phone emissions for his developing multiple sclerosis.[4] This is too large a subject to cover in any depth here; for more information please see my book *A Basic Guide to Technopathic Stress*.[5]

Other studies

In 1989 Austrian researcher Dr Otto Bergsmann began a two-year study at the University of Vienna investigating the short-term consequences of human exposure to pathogenic sites. He noted many significant alterations to biological functions such as changes in the serum values of serotonin, zinc, and calcium in the body after only *ten minutes* exposure to geopathic stress zones. With a large study pool of 985 people and almost 7,000 individual tests completed, this is a well-documented modern study of the phenomenon; sadly, a proper English translation has yet to be published.

A more intensive seven-year study was carried out in Germany between 1988 and 1995 by naturopath Andreas Kopschina with Ursula & Wolfgang Daun. The study, involving 8,200 subjects, measured patients' ability to recover from chronic illness regardless of the type of conventional or integrative therapy being received. The team established that 34% of patients were exposed to significant levels of geopathic stress, leading them to conclude that their capacity to heal was greatly impaired until they were removed from the geopathic structure.

Ulrike Banis, MD, ND, author of *Geopathic Stress - and What You Can Do About It*, has integrated the knowledge of geopathic stress into her medical practice in Bregenz, Austria with categorical success. From her former stance as a staunch sceptic, she now reports,

> *My experience - being a medical professional myself - is that at least 30% of all chronic medical conditions are derived from this cause - or to put it differently, our patients would be, on average, 30% healthier if we manage to find good sleeping places for everyone.*

Dr Banis uses dowsing to identify areas of geopathic stress for her patients. She recommends patients move their sleeping place to an area free of geopathic influence. She then prescribes homeopathic remedies to detox the body of the charge geopathic stress causes within that person's energy field. She even goes as far as to refuse further treatment if the patient won't take preventative measures to ameliorate the geopathic stress!

Schumann Resonance

You will frequently come across Schumann Resonance mentioned as a factor in connection with geopathic stress. It's most often cited by purveyors of expensive 'Schumann Resonator' devices sold to remediate geopathic stress, frequently accompanied by exaggerated claims that said devices will eliminate geopathic stress, protect you from electromagnetic pollution, strengthen your aura, help you sleep better, and so on. One device on the market even claims that it will enhance the sound of your Hi-Fi system! While many of these claims are clearly hyperbole designed to increase sales, there is some science behind it that is worthy of further exploration.

Schumann Resonances (SR) were first conceived and proposed by the German physicist Dr WO Schumann in 1952 and refer to electromagnetic waves generated in the atmospheric cavity between the surface of the Earth and the electrically charged reflective upper atmospheric band known as the ionosphere. The ionosphere is what enables short-wave radio transmissions to be picked up around the world, as it bounces the radio waves back and forth around the globe, allowing them to propagate well beyond the normal line-of-sight transmission range. It also protects the Earth from incoming high-energy solar and cosmic rays. The space between the ionosphere and the Earth's surface acts as a resonant cavity for extremely low frequency (ELF) electromagnetic waves. At any given second, up to one hundred lightning discharges are occurring around the planet. Under the right atmospheric conditions, a standing wave is produced with a base fundamental frequency of approximately 7.83 Hertz, plus several higher harmonics. The Earth is not the only planet to display SR; they have also been observed on Mars, Venus,

Jupiter, and Saturn, as well as Saturn's moon Titan. While they'd been predicted in 1952, Schumann Resonances were first measured reliably in the early 1960s. Since then, scientists have discovered that variations in the resonances correspond to changes in the seasons, solar activity, activity in Earth's magnetic environment, in water aerosols in the atmosphere, and other Earth-bound phenomena.[6]

Because Schumann Resonances have been generated since the formation of the ionosphere, well before animal evolution on Earth, it is theorised that electrical activity in our brains evolved to be in harmony with these frequencies. Furthermore, if the SR frequencies are disrupted or removed, then detrimental physiological and psychological effects are produced in our bodies. It is even widely reported that NASA routinely install Schumann Resonators in spacecraft to keep astronauts healthy, although finding a reliable citation for this piece of apocrypha proves remarkably elusive.

Dr Neil Cherry, former Associate Professor of Environmental Health at Lincoln University in Canterbury, New Zealand, proposed that the SR signal regulates melatonin production in the body, noting strong correlations between the first five harmonics of the Schumann Resonance and the first four human EEG bands below 35Hz:

> Mammals have advanced physiological systems to deal with diurnal and seasonal climate variations. This involves the melatonin/serotonin system communicating with all the vital organs in the body in order to maintain thermal homeostasis. External ULF/ELF signals help to regulate this ... It is highly probable that the Schumann Resonances (SR) provide this signal. It is thus plausible that alteration of the SR signal by Solar and Geomagnetic Activity (S-GMA) is transferred to mammal pineal glands and can

affect their vital organs, especially their brains, CNS, hearts, reproduction and immune systems.

The theoretical, experimental, and observational data involving animals and people gives very strong support for the Schumann Resonance Hypothesis and its Melatonin Mechanism. There is overwhelming evidence that S-GMA is a natural hazard causing reproductive, neurological cardiac and carcinogenic illness and death with cyclic and extreme swings in Solar/Geomagnetic Activity. This is supported with the highly plausible hypothesis that requires only a small amount of confirming research to establish a causal relationship.[7]

This research does lead one to ponder whether human colonisation of other planets is actually possible in the absence of similar SR frequencies on the alien world. If mental activity is so dependent on Schumann Resonance, can humans function at all without it? That's a question I encourage you to dowse for yourself.

The Bottom Line

Spending prolonged periods of time in geopathic disturbance zones – for example, having your bed situated over one – gradually depletes the immune system and make it more difficult for the body to recover from ailments and disease. As we spend the majority of our domestic lives in bed, the bedroom is the obvious first place to check for geopathic stress. Poor sleep patterns and feelings of exhaustion are common first indicators, and the effects are insidious and relentless if left untreated. Of course, office spaces, schools and colleges where the individual is spending most of the day in the same place, such as sitting at the same desk, can also be affected, and, as Bachler's school studies demonstrate, pupils sitting at desks situated over geopathic stress lines have poorer learning scores. Bachler's system of 'rolling classrooms', where desk positions are rotated every few weeks, has a lot to recommend it.

Any good holistic practitioner such as a vibrational homeopath or a health kinesiologist should be able to tell if you are suffering from geopathic stress. Many bio-resonance tools such as the Lecher antenna, Vega, Mora, and Asyra devices can be used to assess geopathic stress levels in the human energy field. It is in the practitioner's interest to check for this as geopathic stress will interfere with the body's natural healing processes and reduce the effectiveness of their treatments. Of course dowsing can also reveal the presence of geopathic stress, but working in conjunction with a holistic practitioner is an ideal way to assess your dowsing performance in this field, as you get feedback on your work when the client next visits their health practitioner.

Chapter 4

Shamanic Cosmology

If you want to learn about nature, to appreciate nature, it is necessary to understand the language that she speaks in.

-- RICHARD FEYNMAN

There are some realms of the human psyche that are difficult for even the most advanced dowser to explore if they have no personal experience of those areas. No amount of book reading or workshops can prepare you for what an out-of-body experience feels like, or what visions and insights will result from the ingestion of a psychoactive teacher plant like ayahuasca, for instance. These alternative realities are nigh-impossible to describe. We can try, but the experiences are beyond language and our words become meaningless. They must be experienced directly, and the information processed into our own personal picture of reality. That's why these transcendent events are called 'the Mysteries' in traditional occult schools. Over the centuries countless esoteric researchers have explored these alternative realities. From tribal shamans, trance mediums, alchemists, ceremonial magicians, witches, Buddhists and yogis to the casual experimenter 'tripping' with psychoactive plants - all have returned with their own visions of what the 'outside' looks like from their point of view. Everyone's experience will be unique and personal, but luckily there are some universal archetypes, common across cultures, that have been passed down in myths, folklore, and legends. Having some knowledge of these archetypes, and recognising them when they are encountered, enables the valiant shaman to arrange them into a mental 'road map' that will become more detailed through further experience. Such a road map may also prove useful to the intrepid dowser working in the spirit realms and, although your own reality model will inevitably be moulded by your personal spiritual background and cultural upbringing, you may find some nuggets of value in the following.

The World Tree

One of the most common cosmological models found in ancient cultures is the idea of three 'worlds' or 'realms' – the Upper (abode of the gods), Middle (earth), and Lower (the Underworld, realm of the dead). We see some residual echoes of this today in Christian theology, where Heaven is thought of as 'above' and Hell is somewhere 'below'. The early Egyptian peoples ascribed the Upper World to the goddess Nut, whose body was the night sky, the Earth to her brother and mate Geb, and the Underworld to the dog-headed god Anubis, although he was later demoted to gatekeeper in favour of Geb's son Osiris. Babylonian cosmology was similar, although they had two heavens and two underworlds. Greek and Roman myths, which largely developed from the earlier Babylonian stories, tried to anchor the tales more in the physical realm by locating the gods atop a high mountain and access to the underworld through caves, but the basic idea is the same.

The three-world model is perhaps best expounded in Norse mythology. We inhabit Middle Earth, or *Midgard* The Upper

World, or land of the Gods (*Asgard*) is above, and underneath is the Underworld (*Hel*), the Realm of the Dead. The mighty ash tree *Yggdrasil* grows in the centre, connecting the three worlds with its trunk. The fully developed Norse cosmogony actually contains nine realms, but for our purposes we need only concern ourselves with these three.

The antiquarian Hilda Ellis Davidson notes parallels between Yggdrasil and shamanic lore in northern Eurasia:

> *The conception of the tree rising through a number of worlds is found in northern Eurasia and forms part of the shamanic lore shared by many peoples of this region. This seems to be a very ancient conception, perhaps based on the Pole Star, the centre of the heavens, and the image of the central tree in Scandinavia may have been influenced by it.... Among Siberian shamans, a central tree may be used as a ladder to ascend the heavens.[1]*

This idea of a central *axis mundi* is something of a universal archetype, probably dating back to the dawn of time when our Palaeolithic ancestors sat in a circle around their campfire to keep the night at bay - the whole of their visible reality at that moment defined by the circle of light cast by the flames. The association with the Pole Star is a profound concept, as ancient people could not help but notice the heavens revolving around a fixed point in the sky. This naturally evokes the idea of a wheel revolving on an axle, and one can't help wondering if it was this very observation that led to the invention of the wheel. (Note that due to precession - the approximately 26,000 year 'wobble' of the Earth's axis - the designated pole star changes. Some 5,000 years ago, the star Thuban in the constellation of Draco was the star closest to the north celestial pole. Currently, it is Polaris in Ursa Minor, and in another 4,000 years it will be Alderamin in the constellation Cepheus).

The image of a circle with its central point marked is a powerful symbol, so much so that it is the universal symbol for the Sun, the ultimate source of all life on Earth. A circle can be mathematically defined as 'an infinite number of points equidistant from a centre', and it is the first manifestation of form in sacred geometry. Draw a circle around yourself and you immediately distinguish your personal space from your surroundings. By turning in a circle with a finger pointing outwards, you define your own personal horizon. That's really the power of the circle. It is the first expression of Universe; a horizon, a boundary between Self and Other. The circle in its manifestation implies the divine generation of shape and form from nothing to everything.

In our personal circles, we need to know where our centre is at all times and on all levels. In meditation, and when dowsing for that matter, we speak of being 'grounded' and 'centred' before beginning work. It is our mental protocol to establish our core – our personal axis mundi - and provides a fixed frame of reference for us to return to when necessary. It is always important to ground and centre yourself before doing any advanced dowsing work, particularly when dowsing in the spiritual realms that we shall be discussing later. We'll look at protection protocols in the next chapter.

We have an inherent need to establish this axis mundi in all areas of our lives. The campfire of the ancients has been replaced by the hearth as our living spaces developed. Initially, the fire was central in Iron Age crannogs and roundhouses, and in the tents and yurts of nomadic tribes, or Native American tipis. With more permanent dwellings, the hearth was moved to the side of the main living space, but it remained a central focus until comparatively recent times. Nowadays the central focus of a room is more likely to be the television.

I noticed a profound shift in the feng-shui of my own living room when I replaced a rectangular coffee table with a circular one crafted from an old cartwheel - the room immediately developed its own axis mundi around the table, and movement of people and energy became much more fluid and natural.

Many of our villages and towns were planned around a central location, which may have been the mercat (market) cross (Fig. 9), the tron (municipal scales), or even the main square, town hall or post office. Of course, this had a very practical purpose in providing a place for people to assemble for trade, fairs, town meetings, dispensing of justice, official pronouncements and so on. Often this central point is ceremonially

Figure 9: Mercat cross, Doune

created as part of the act of foundation of the town, with a stone or other marker defining this *omphalos* (navel) - see for example, the London Stone, thought by some to have been placed there by the Romans as the central *milliarium*, the point from which all distances in Roman Britain were measured.[2]

The concept has been taken to the extreme in Dublin, where the city installed a massive 121m metal spike in the centre of O'Connell Street in 2003, on the former site of the  Nelson Pillar, which was destroyed by a bomb attack in 1966. Although informally called the 'Millennium Spire' (Fig. 10), the wry Dublin sense of humour has resulted in its more colloquial sobriquet of the 'Stiletto in the Ghetto'. Claimed as the world's largest sculpture, the Monument of Light, to give it its proper name, is truly an axis mundi of epic proportion and it quite

Figure 10: Millennium Spire literally connects earth and sky, forming an energy conduit between the two. This is a powerful geomantic act of foundation, exactly analogous to the way a geomancer will use a wooden or metal stake, megalith or other device in ceremony to fix the serpentine currents of earth energy in place, before constructing a sacred structure in order to harness those qualities for the space – an act known as 'pinning the dragon'. The geomancer is creating the axis mundi for that particular space. This may be the hidden truth behind the origin stories of St Michael, St George and other dragon-slaying saints.

There is more to this geomantic connection between earth and sky as provided by the spire. There is a very real energy exchange between the spire and the air, particularly during thunderstorms when the electrical potential difference between the top and bottom of the structure can be in the order of several tens of thousands of volts per cubic centimetre. The tip of the spike radiates positively charged ions into the atmosphere, which tends to attract lightning, and indeed the Spire has been hit by lightning on several occasions. Fortunately, the structure is well grounded internally and there is therefore no danger to the public in the event of a strike. High electrical potential in the atmosphere can also result in the peculiar phenomenon known as St Elmo's fire, a blue or purplish glow in the air around the monument's point. Any pointed object will produce positive ions at the tip, and St Elmo's Fire can also occur on sailing boats where the height and small profile of the mast acts in a comparable fashion.

The spires of churches serve a remarkably similar function in ensuing the transfer of energy between earth and sky, and in a geomantically-constructed space where the building is sited on a harmonious confluence of earth energies and underground water flows, this subtle energy transfer is enhanced, helping to maintain and energise the space. In older churches with spires, you can usually dowse a blind spring (water dome) directly underneath the spire. The rising water generates a discontinuity in the geomagnetic field, producing a vortex of energy that is channelled and shaped by the spire above, enhancing the electrical exchange between the tip of the spire and the surrounding atmosphere. In particularly charged atmospheric conditions, this can even manifest as lightning strikes.

The Axis of Consciousness

In our shamanic model, the trunk of the World Tree provides a personal axis mundi, representing a conceptual pillar that we can think of as an axis of consciousness. Our highest ideals and aspirations are situated towards the top of the tree, while our foundation, subconscious, and the lower shadow aspects of ourselves – the stuff we would rather not face - are located amongst the roots. The topmost branches connect to our Higher Selves and beyond to Deity, Source - whatever your personal idea of Highest Universal Intelligence is - whilst the roots burrow deep into the darkest areas of our soul, the realm of the Ancestors and of the Dead. You can also think of the trunk in terms of an axis of frequency rather like a radio spectrum, with higher frequencies at the top and lower ones at the bottom (Fig. 11). [3]

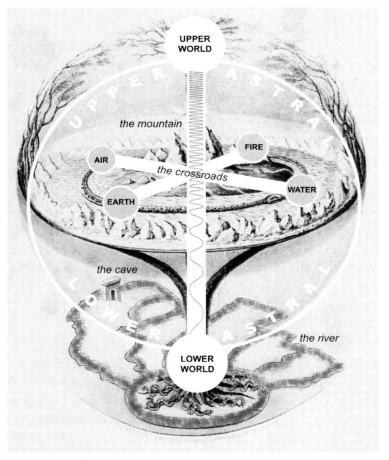

Figure 11: The World Tree

The Directions and the Elements

Middle Earth, the central plane of the Tree, represents our normal everyday consciousness. We stand at the centre, at what we can call the Crossroads. Crossroads are a common metaphor in folk magic and mythology; the symbol of the cross represents the intersection of spirit and matter, or heaven and earth, so the Crossroads is a place where two realms meet. It is a liminal place 'between the worlds', where spirits can manifest and other magical events occur. In folklore, crossroads are often depicted as places where pacts between man and demon are struck, for example in the Faust story where the demon Mephistopheles is summoned at a crossroads. Or there is the tale of legendary blues singer Robert Johnson, who allegedly sold his soul to the Devil at a crossroads at midnight in return for his guitar-playing ability. In the Middle Ages, it was the custom to bury criminals, suicides, and suspected vampires at crossroads, in the belief that the multiple roads would confuse the spirit and prevent them from returning to haunt the living.

All these tales serve to reinforce the idea that the Crossroads is a 'no-place', somewhere outside of everyday reality. It is a focal point of manifestation. Surrounding us are the four Directions, each with their own correspondences - element, colour, governing spirit, Tarot suit and so on. Every action that we take, every decision that we make, is a step towards one of the Directions and is 'flavoured' by that particular element. So, for instance, we might be angry about something or annoyed with someone - this takes us in the direction of Fire. Or we might be highly emotional about something, which would be the direction of Water, and so on. These concepts are so grounded in our everyday consciousness that even though we are not consciously aware of it we unwittingly weave them into our language and behaviour. For example, we might speak of 'getting our fingers burned' if we venture into the realm of Fire and interfere with something that we shouldn't, or we might talk of someone having a 'fiery personality' if they are prone to outbursts of anger.

Fire is the element associated with sight, creative thought, and our drive to get things done. It is generative energy in its most primal form with the potential for both creation and destruction. In the Tarot, the suit of Wands is traditionally associated with Fire, and in the magick circle it is located in the south, the direction of the mid-day sun.[4] In the shamanic worldview, the elemental guardians of Fire are salamanders. This is a well-established association in the folklore of many cultures and may originate from a behaviour common to several species of salamander, who hibernate under rotting logs. When such wood was brought indoors and burned, the creatures appeared, as if by magic, from the flames. It was also thought that the milky substance that salamanders exude when frightened, making their skin moist, gave rise to the idea that the salamander could withstand extremes of heat and even extinguish fires with their secretions. Salamanders are even mentioned in the *Talmud,* where they are described as creatures that are the product of fire, and that anyone who is smeared with salamander blood will be immune to fire.[5]

The Realm of Air is the domain of the Sylphs. These unpredictable sprites have long been popular in the Arts, inspiring the 'airy spirits' in Shakespeare's *A Midsummer Night's Dream* and by extension the spirit Ariel in *The Tempest;* and then of course there are the great 19th century Classical ballets, Bournonville's *La Sylphide*

and Fokine's *Les Sylphides* (the former brilliantly updated for contemporary audiences in Matthew Bourne's 1994 *Highland Fling*). There are clear overlaps with early Victorian depictions of gossamer-winged fairies and even the *devas* of Theosophy and New Age tradition. The term sylph is thought to have been originally coined by physician and alchemist Paracelsus in the 16th century as part of his classifications of the four elements, although he was clearly drawing on much older sources. These names were soon adopted and widely disseminated in subsequent Hermetic literature.[6]

We might say of a person who has difficulty focusing on tasks that they 'have their head in the clouds', or are 'away with the fairies', or have an 'airy-fairy' personality. Or perhaps this is a rather 'lightweight' analogy (if you'll pardon the pun)? In the body, Air is associated with the sensations of smell and taste, and it is the medium of communication, as sound waves require air to propagate. It also represents the intellect, logical reasoning and thought in general. The Tarot suit associated with Air is that of Swords, as the cutting action of the sword is analogous to the act of decision-making. Air is something that we tend to take for granted as it is invisible and seldom felt, yet is absolutely fundamental to our continued existence on this planet. Its correspondence with knowledge and the intellect means that Air is the element associated with the traditional idea of the 'Akashic Records', which posits the existence of a great astral repository of all knowledge, events and memory of past lives both personal and universal, which in meditation is symbolically seen as a huge library. A more contemporary association would be the Jungian 'collective unconscious', although it's more fashionable nowadays to refer to this as the 'information field'.

 There are many phrases in common usage that relate to the element of Water. If we are overwhelmed by emotion, we may say that we are 'drowning in sorrow' or describe a particularly dolorous individual as being 'a bit of a wet blanket', 'soppy', or a 'bit of a drip'. As our bodies consist of around 60% water, it is not surprising that this element has such a huge influence on our behaviour. Water is life, it nourishes us and infuses everything around us. Esoterically, anything that flows belongs under the aegis of Water. Because of its ability to dissolve many substances, water is regarded as a universal carrier medium and as such is responsible for the manifestation of our senses in the other elemental realms. It is the element of emotions, both positive and negative. Positive emotions lift our frequency upwards towards the top of the tree, whereas intense negative emotions tend to get repressed into the Underworld at the roots of the tree, where they infect the base of our being until we deal with them. Because of this, Water is the most frequently used elemental realm with which to access the Underworld. The most commonly found symbolism here is the well, lake, river, or sea. While wells and lakes may be used to descend into the Underworld, rivers are often used to mark the boundaries between the different realms, as they represent psychological crossing points. The Tarot suit associated with Water is that of Cups or Chalices.

It is perhaps no coincidence that Celtic peoples were known for throwing weapons into lakes and rivers as offerings; as these liminal boundaries were thought of as portals to the Underworld. This seems particularly obvious on a clear night when the infinity of stars overhead is reflected in still water. Who has not stood on a river bridge, a seaside clifftop, or on the stern of a ship gazing into the fast-flowing waters below and not felt the urge to jump in? You are feeling the very tangible pull of the water spirits.

The denizens of this realm have many names - naiads, nereids, sea sprites, mermaids; but they fall under the general term of Undines.[7] These playful spirits, who are almost always female, have likewise inspired many works of literature, ballet, drama and music, for example the character of Melisande from *Pelléas et Mélisande,* which has appeared as play, poem and several musical versions. Frederick Ashton famously choreographed the ballet *Undine* for Margot Fonteyn, and of course there is the ever-popular Hans Christian Anderson tale modernised for our own time as Disney's *The Little Mermaid.*

 The Realm of Earth is that of material reality, providing our experience of solid matter, form, and substance. We are closer to the realm of Earth than any other as we are physical beings and live our lives on the earth, so we have many aphorisms relating to it. We speak of somebody being very 'down to earth', having their 'feet on the ground', or possessing an 'earthy humour', we might feel 'grounded' or 'heavy' and so on. I'm sure there are many other similar examples that you can think of. The Tarot suit associated with this element is Pentacles, which symbolise material exchange, money, possessions, business, and commerce.

The elemental Beings of Earth are the Gnomes. These diminutive builders and craft persons oversee all growing things as well as the movements of rock and soil. Gnomes are nowadays quite ensconced in everyday consciousness, as evidenced by the popularity of the garden gnome in all its varieties. They can often be clairvoyantly perceived during quiet meditation in nature, where you might get a glimpse of a gnome in the negative space between leaves on a shrub or flower. American geomancer Marty Cain[8] teaches that we each have two personal gnomes who remain with us throughout our lives, with responsibility to creatively interfere with our lives 'for the highest good'. Although generally of a cheerful disposition, gnomes enjoy mischief and humorous pranks that can be mildly irritating at times. Hiding things from you when you really need to find the item is typical gnome behaviour. But if you can't find your car keys when you really need to leave the house, it's probably for your own good as you might have been involved in an accident if you had left at your intended time. They mean well and have your best interests at heart.

Gnomes are excellent gardeners and can teach you a lot about the plants and flowers in your garden. During a gnomes workshop with Marty Cain in Chalice Well Gardens in Glastonbury (where I was doing my geomancy training with Sig Lonegren and Patrick MacManaway), having tuned in and contacted my gnomes using my pendulum, I asked them to show me an interesting plant in the gardens by using a single L-rod as direction finder. After a few minutes following where the rod led me, I was taken off the footpath into a corner where there was a clutch of *arum maculatum* plants (Lords-and-Ladies or Cuckoo Pint). These plants with their obvious sexual symbolism and dark-spotted leaves are quite common around Glastonbury but were new to me at the time; I discovered their significance in a later session that same day where Sig referred to them as the 'Magdalene plant', regarding them as emblematic of the divine feminine. This because Mary Magdalene is traditionally regarded as a temple prostitute or 'fallen woman', and *maculatum* in Latin means stained, defiled, or dishonoured. Apparently, my gnomes knew what was going on better than I did!

Gnomes are also very fond of labyrinths, and personal experience has taught me that it always pays to acknowledge not only your own gnomes, but those of other people working with you, when building a labyrinth. This helps to avoid the moment of confusion that invariably seems to arise during the construction of one. On one of my early labyrinth builds using cobbles, I was laying out the stones as three other people were ferrying them to me, but nothing was going well – stones were dropped, the wrong ones selected, fingers were getting bashed, my marking-out string kept getting tangled with my compass cord... it was a complete mess. Then I tuned in and apologised for not involving the gnomes of everyone and asked them to forgive us and help us finish the labyrinth, whereupon everything suddenly fell into place and we finished the construction without further ado and in short order. It always pays to be nice to your gnomes!

Whether these beings I am describing have any objective reality or not is a matter for debate, and you may feel that this talk of gnomes, salamanders and the like is no more than childish nonsense. Yet these ideas lie at the heart of Western magical tradition and are archetypal concepts to those of us brought up in western societies. Other cultures will have their own equivalents and may feel more comfortable working in a framework rooted in their own experience. We must remember that these terms have been passed down to us from our ancestors, and their view of reality was not as scientifically developed as that of our own. We are using these non-scientific, medieval-sounding terms to describe mental forces, qualities, feelings, ideas, or *aspects of consciousness* that we have no proper terms of reference for, and you may find it helpful to think of them like that. You do not have to believe in them as objectively real; instead, say, "Here is a particular quality of earth energy that I am calling a gnome" (or troll, or fairy, or whatever). Just as you don't need to know how the cake tastes to follow a recipe, so you don't need to believe in the physical reality of these beings in order to work with them. Over time, you will develop a sense of how they present themselves to you and will learn to distinguish one aspect of the earth force from another. It's not something that can be taught or learned from reading a book. These things have to be experienced and interpreted personally, and you may end up using different terms to describe them according to your own background and personal belief system. This is absolutely fine.

Upper World

Middle Earth is the realm of experience and describes the physical world. Surrounding this on the World Tree, we find the numinous layers of the Astral Plane, or what we might call in today's parlance, the *information field*. In the Upper Astral (we might say at higher *frequencies*), we encounter the realm of ideas and concepts. This is the domain of the ego in Jungian psychology. I like to think of the upper astral as the 'design shop' for reality, where stuff is prototyped before manifesting in the physical. Like any big industrial workshop, the astral can be a chaotic place. It has lots of bits and pieces being worked on, a large workforce of various beings working in both managerial and blue-collar roles, and lots of half-baked, failed, and unfinished projects lying around littering the floor, complete with the unwanted vermin and bugs that such rubbish tends to attract. This Lower Astral dross can attach to the unwary traveller and is often responsible for minor psychospiritual disturbances in the home. Sensitive individuals may even unwittingly 'call in' entities - pubescent children are frequently associated with cases of poltergeist activity for example. Dowsers working with these energies should check that they are well-protected.

In our dreams, our astral selves travel in this realm, picking up impressions and half-formed concepts from the Upper Astral that sometimes carry over to the waking world, providing inspiration to artists, writers, composers, and other creatives. Several composers have described waking up in the morning with a fully-formed song or orchestral work in their head – Mozart was particularly known for this, and the electrical genius Nikola Tesla frequently awoke with complete designs for new apparatus. But this need not be a random occurrence during sleep - a consciously directed intention can create and mould these astral ideas before they are manifested in the physical realm. It is a meditative process described by Jung as *active imagination*, where the contents of the unconscious mind are translated into images and narrative, or personified as separate entities. The process creates a bridge between our subconscious and conscious minds, allowing the subconscious to express itself without overbearing influence from the conscious mind. By allowing the developing scene to unfold naturally in our imagination whilst maintaining detachment from it, we can reflect on any changes and respond accordingly to subtly influence the results as desired. Jung put it like this: "You yourself must enter into the process with your personal reactions ... as if the drama being enacted before your eyes were real".[9] Our belief structure creates a filter through which chaos is sifted into order. In the language of quantum mechanics, we are *collapsing the wave function*. This is the very essence of magickal (and geomancy) work. It how we focus our intention to initiate the desired change.

The higher astral frequencies merge into what Jungian psychologists refer to as the 'superconscious'. This area is only seldom accessed by normal human awareness, and then mostly by adepts in deep meditation. This is the domain of our higher selves, our guardian angels and our spirit guides, and is where the idea of the 'dowsing source' comes from. Beyond this lies the unknowable realm of the divine consciousness, Great Spirit, God, Goddess... whatever your perception of the highest intelligence of Nature happens to be. Everything here is perceived from below through the filter of our ego, so our concept of these energies is shaped by the forms that our human consciousness applies in order to comprehend it. This is a crucial point, accounting for the wide variety of gods and goddesses, and indeed the entire panoply of world religions. Every prophet forges their own path to the top of the mountain, yet ultimately, they all arrive at the same place. How they bring that vision back down the mountain depends on their ego filter.

Although we cannot access these highest frequencies directly and may only get occasional glimpses of them in the deepest meditation; we can still use our dowsing ability to seek answers from here by working through our spirit guides, higher selves, or dowsing sources – whatever you choose to call 'it'. The renowned earth energy dowser Hamish Miller used to refer to 'it' as, 'the Management'; others simply call it 'Upstairs'.

Lower World

Descending the Tree brings us to the realm of the Underworld, which corresponds with the Personal Unconscious in Jungian psychology. It can be a dark and fearful place. This is where we store all our fears, suppressed emotions, and darker elements of self that we are not willing to face. These rejected aspects of personality, if not acknowledged and confronted, can develop into personal demons that cause real psychological problems. In meditation or shamanic journeying, we can venture into this shadowy realm with the aid of a psychopomp (guide) to help us navigate. This is usually your power animal, generally visualised as a real animal and rarely, a snake or dragon.

In shamanic journeying, various doorways are available to access the Underworld, commonly through the elements of Water or Earth. For Water, meditations involving a dark pool or a well can be used. Descending into a cave or crawling into an animal burrow between the roots of a tree are effective entry points from the Earth plane. Think of Lewis Carroll's *Alice's Adventures in Wonderland*, where Alice is guided into her Underworld by her psychopomp guide, the White Rabbit; this can be seen as a thinly-veiled account of an Underworld shamanic journey. The Cave is arguably the easiest and most commonly used portal into the Lower World, as our bodies consist of matter and we spend our lives on the material plane, so we are closest in nature to the element of Earth.

The Unconscious is often likened to a river in psychology, and in our three-world model, we find a many-branched river flowing around the roots of the Tree, each tributary leading to different areas of the Underworld. The rivers act as liminal boundaries to separate each aspect or area of experience. In dreams, the act of crossing a river represents a huge change in circumstance, overcoming burdens and obstacles. Such dreams usually accompany a major life change.

The Classical psychopomp of the River is of course, Charon the ferryman, who traditionally guides the souls of the dead across the River Styx. Here, we come to the lowest frequency of consciousness, positioned beyond the Underworld, the realm of the Ancestors or the Collective Unconscious in Jungian terms. In every culture, it is a realm of danger and terror, with disturbing imagery. This is the true realm of the dead and is so far removed from our waking reality that we cannot access it directly while living. Advanced meditators may be able to stand on the bank of the River and get a glimpse of the other side, but Charon's services are reserved solely for those souls who have departed the physical plane.

Chapter 5
Ethics and Protection

Until you make the unconscious conscious, it will direct your life and you will call it fate.

- CARL JUNG

Any advanced remedial dowsing work is essentially more of a shamanic practise, as we focus our intent to bring healing to the situation. *Where intention goes, energy flows.* Accordingly, we need to be more aware of our personal energetic space and psychic hygiene. Although the basic 3-question, *"Can I? May I? Should I?"* protocol is sufficient for most investigatory dowsing, for advanced work it is advisable that we pay more attention to our own protection.

Whether we are working with the landscape or healing a building space, we need to adjust our own vibrational frequency to be in *resonance* with the space that we are working with. Imagine that you have two radios, each tuned to a slightly different frequency, one above a broadcasting station, the other slightly below it. Each radio, if the frequency is close enough, may pick up a faint and distorted signal of the radio station, but neither will receive a clear transmission. Both radios will need tuning adjusted until they are the same in order to clearly receive the station; one radio needs to tune to a lower frequency, the other to tune upwards until they are both at the correct frequency. A similar thing happens between two people at the start of a relationship. Interaction between them can be a little disjointed in the beginning, but over time as their 'tuning' adjusts, both come into resonance and clear communication results. You may have noticed when you have spent a period of time away from your partner or family that this 'resonance' needs to be regained on your return; miscommunications and minor arguments seem common and often it takes a day or two for domestic harmony to be restored.

I encourage you to look up 'Barton's Pendulum' on the internet.[1] This is an experiment first invented by Edwin Henry Barton (1858-1925), who was Professor of Physics at University College, Nottingham. In the experiment, a number of pendulums of different lengths are hung from a common string, with one heavier 'driver' pendulum at the end. When the driver pendulum is started swinging, the other pendulums will begin to move in varying swings, with the one closest in length to the driver pendulum developing the greatest amplitude of swing. These two pendulums are in *resonance*. Exactly the same principle applies when we are working to assess and bring healing to a space. We need to adjust our own 'frequency' to bring ourselves into resonance with the subject. In this way, we open a clear channel of communication, and our dowsing responses will be more accurate. The trick is to do this without leaving ourselves open to any detrimental forces; hence we need to introduce some protective measures.

The basic requirements of psychic protection are simple; we wish to strengthen our energy field - the aura - so that it becomes a barrier that prevents unwanted psychic and spiritual energies from affecting us. At the same time however, in order to do the work, we need to 'open up' our psychic senses so that they can detect any abnormalities in the energy field of the subject. Let's suppose that you have lived your entire life in a completely closed room with no doors or windows, just four solid walls and roof. You have no idea what, if anything, exists beyond the walls of your room. Then one day, you hear noises through the walls, the first clue suggesting the presence of something external. How do you find out what the source is? The most obvious method is to cut some holes into the walls to make windows. Now you can see out, the light can get in, and you see the source of the noise. What if it's a swarm of bees, or a large unfriendly-looking animal? Or maybe it's cold and blowing a blizzard outside. How do you stop it coming through the holes into your room? Well, you could install some glass in your windows of course. Now you can continue to see outside, while at the same time keeping out any unwanted influences. Psychic protection is a bit like that - it's the reinforced extra-tempered super-safety double or triple glazing that you install in the 'windows' of your aura to stop unwanted influences from getting in. It's not a total barrier - you don't want to block everything out – rather, it's a filtering mechanism that you can mentally 'tune' to allow helpful and beneficial energies through whilst keeping out anything nasty. You set the parameters that control what to let in and what to keep out.

Some dowsers argue that additional protection is unnecessary, because the very act of dowsing has its own built-in safeguards and that is defence enough; however, my argument is that it's better to have extra protection and not require it than not to have it and then find yourself in a situation where you actually need it. You wouldn't go outside in the snow on a winter's day without putting on a heavy coat and boots; nor should you do shamanic dowsing work without taking some additional precautions. It's only common sense. It doesn't make us less sensitive; it provides us with more control. At the very least, the act of going through a protection protocol helps to get you properly into your 'dowsing zone' and is arguably better than doing nothing at all.

Advanced Dowsing Protocol

There are of course, many methods of protection, and you may already have a preferred technique depending on your cultural background and belief system. If this is the case, then feel free to skip ahead to the next chapter. If not, then this is an advanced protocol that I use. It has evolved over the years to become more comprehensive, yet once learned it can be performed quickly in just a minute or two.

First stage

The first stage in any protection routine is to bring yourself physically fully into the present. Give yourself a shake to loosen up any tense muscles, then either stand still or sit comfortably with both feet on the ground. Take a deep breath and let it out as you close your eyes and relax your shoulders.

Become aware of the rhythm of your breathing; don't force it into any particular pattern, just be aware of it. Now imagine that the Sun is directly overhead. As you breathe in, imagine a shaft of light descending from the Sun and entering your head, passing down your body into your heart chakra. Feel a ball of light growing there, spreading out into a football-sized sphere. As you breathe out, extend the column of light down into the Earth.

Keep repeating this, breathing in the light from above, feeling the light in your chest growing brighter, breathing out the light into the Earth. Feel your feet becoming heavier the more you do this.

Keep doing this until you feel that the light you are sending downwards has reached the very centre of the Earth. You might feel some sort of 'ping' or colour sensation, get an image of a large crystal, or something else entirely, but you will sense that it has reached there. When that happens, change the pattern of your breathing.

Now, as you breathe in, bring the light both down from the Sun and upwards from the centre of the Earth into your heart chakra. As you breathe out, imagine that the ball of light in your chest is expanding, becoming larger with each breath as it grows to fill your body with the clear white light. Keep doing this and visualise the light expanding out beyond the confines of your body to fill your entire aura with sparkling light. Most people see the aura as an egg-shaped field of energy, usually white, but gold or a neon-blue colour is also popular. At this point, you can consider yourself to be fully grounded and centred, connected to both Upper World and Lower World, functioning as the intermediary between both Worlds. Mentally bring your focus back to your body, keeping the image of the shining shell of energy around you.

This grounding and protection exercise is something that can be done relatively quickly with practice. In just the space of a few deep breaths you can be peaceful, centred, and clear in yourself and the psychically defined space that you have created around you.

Second Stage

Mentally invoke (connect with) your highest ideals, whether they be your concept of Divinity, Mother Nature, Great Mystery, the Flying Spaghetti Monster or whatever. With your pendulum swinging in the 'search' pattern, mentally affirm something like, "*I ask to be connected to the Divine spirit and in resonance with the highest intelligence and beneficial energies of Nature. I ask to be protected and guided by my Spirit Team and that my dowsing be 100% accurate"* (If you are not consciously aware of your spirit guides, don't worry - they're still there for you and appreciate being asked!). You don't need to use that exact affirmation, feel free to make up something of your own that has more personal relevance for you.

Your pendulum should be giving you one or more 'yes' responses during this part of the procedure. If it's not, you can come back to this stage and repeat it after stage four.

This is also where you can ask for assistance from other spirit helpers, so if you work with angels for instance, you will call them in at this stage. Sometimes you will become aware of other beings willing to assist. These may manifest to you as a mental picture that jumps into your head, or perhaps a feeling, sensation, or even a physical noise from a passing bird or animal. You can of course also ask if there are any nature spirits, elementals or other geomantic beings willing to support you in your work, checking with your pendulum to ensure that they are acting in accordance with your highest ideals for the task ahead. Do not connect with anything else!

Third Stage

Next, we need to balance our personal energy fields to ensure that we are fully in the 'dowsing zone'. We can do this by employing our pendulum in the 'decrease/minimise - increase/maximise' technique discussed in *Dowsing Magic - Book 1* and in the companion workbook *Dowsing with Sigils*.

First, we remove any non-beneficial or detrimental energies. Start your pendulum swinging vigorously in your 'decrease/minimise' motion (for me, this is an anticlockwise direction, the same as my 'no' response). As you do this, imagine that any detrimental energy is draining out of you into the earth. Visualise an oscillating screen or sieve of light descending from above your head and proceeding down through your aura, filtering out anything non-beneficial as it goes. It helps to include a spoken affirmation with this; perhaps something along the lines of, "*I ask that the frequencies of any detrimental energies in all parts of my energy field be scrambled, neutralised, and removed from all aspects of my being, and that the energy be transformed for the best and highest good of all things as appropriate for this task...*"

Continue with this visualisation and repeat the affirmation and visualisation as necessary until your pendulum changes its swing or stops. This indicates that you have completed this part and can move on to the next stage.

Fourth Stage

Now, we do the same in reverse. Start the pendulum vigorously swinging in your increase/maximise direction (for me, a clockwise circle (Fig.12), the same as my 'yes' response), meanwhile imagining that clear light is flooding into your energy

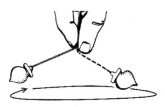

Figure 12: Increase/maximise

field from above and filling up your aura until you are positively burgeoning with sparkling energy and surrounded by a glowing egg-shaped aura. The affirmation to make while doing this should be something like, "*I ask that my energy levels be maximised as appropriate and in harmony with the highest intelligence of Nature and all creation, and that every aspect of my being exists in perfect health...*". Again, you can make up your own affirmation here if you prefer.

As before, you should repeat this affirmation and continue the visualisation until your pendulum changes its swing or stops, indicating that you are ready to proceed.

Using your pendulum in this way is a good technique to adopt in any situation that requires you to work for an unspecified length of time, such as sending healing energy to a client.

If you did not get a definite dowsing response during any of the previous stages, now is the time to go back and repeat that step in the procedure.

Fifth Stage

You should now be well into your 'dowsing zone' and ready to begin work. This is the point to ask your usual three, "Can I? May I? Should I?" questions (*Do I have the ability for this task? Do I have all the necessary permissions for this task? Is it timely and appropriate for me to do this now, is there anything I have missed?*). These connect you with the task at hand and ensure that you have covered all the bases and haven't missed anything important. A good additional question to ask here is, "*Am I safe?*" This is like a final 'systems check' to make sure that the preceding stages of the protocol have all been effective. It is important that you maintain your clarity of consciousness and purity of intent throughout the remainder of the dowsing operation.

These five stages are the basis of many advanced dowsing protocols, and you can of course adapt things to suit your own needs and beliefs. Some people will add other affirmations, others might like to place more emphasis on God (or other deity of choice), and so on. The important thing is that you have to feel as if something is happening as you picture the energy flows and say the affirmations. Don't just waggle your pendulum and expect the rest to happen automatically. The pendulum is only an instrument that registers change in a system, in this case indicating when you can move on to the next stage. My Canadian colleague Susan Collins has a very comprehensive procedure that she will be happy to email to you on request. Just drop her a note at susan@dowser.ca with 'protocol' in the subject line.

There may be situations where you simply don't have the time to run through the full protection protocol. For those situations, you can try creating a mental 'macro', which is a very condensed version of the protocol. Once you have run through the protocol several times and are familiar with it, mentally picture yourself going through it in super high-speed mode and visualise the effects of it as you do so. Feel the energetic changes, feel your breathing slowing, feel your sense of the environment sharpen, and so on. Now affirm to yourself that this super-fast protocol is going to happen every time you utter a particular key phrase. I like to say, "Engage dowsing mode GO!", but the phrase can be whatever you prefer. As you speak (or think) the code phrase, mentally see yourself running the protocol and feel it take effect. This is a good shortcut to employ if you are pushed for time, although you should always try to do the full protocol if you can, as it really does help you get into the dowsing zone.

Now that you are prepared for the dowsing task ahead, we can look at some healing techniques. Steps three and four in the protocol can be used to balance energy in many dowsing situations, such as balancing the energy field of your subject, removing detrimental energy and placing protection around a person or object, or performing a remote healing on a house or other space, just by going through the decrease/minimise and increase/maximise stages with appropriate affirmations and visualisations. It's all about focusing your intention here. You are not just twirling your pendulum and wishing for something to happen; you need to really focus on the desired result and strongly visualise it actually happening.

The Dowsing Task

Throughout the entire dowsing process, it is important that you maintain this quality of consciousness until complete. You need to act from a heart-centred state of grace, desiring only to bring balance and harmony to the situation. Remember that dowsing works best when you are in a state of ignorance and apathy. You don't know the answer, and you don't care what it is. Make no prior assumptions about the result and keep your questions as clear and as literal as possible. Inaccurate dowsing usually results from asking vague questions. We dowse in service for others, not for personal gain. I have yet to hear of a dowser getting rich by correctly dowsing lottery numbers – although I'm sure there are many who have tried! It is exceedingly difficult to get accurate answers when dowsing future events, as the future is mutable, and circumstances may change. It may, however, be helpful to dowse the *probability* of a specific event taking place, and for this you can use a simple plus/minus percentage chart. So, for example, if your client asks, "What happens if I do ...", you can tell them that dowsing suggests a certain percentage of probability if they choose that course of action, and so on. But the choice has to be theirs – your job as a dowser is to lay out the probabilities and options for them to make an informed decision, not to make that decision for them.

Always keep your dowsing ethical and don't dowse personal information about someone else without their express permission unless it is clearly in the interest of the highest common good to do so. It is rude and unprofessional to do otherwise. If you want to be respected as a dowser, you must earn that respect by being scrupulously honest about what you are doing and what your client can expect from you. Honest and trustworthy behaviour should be paramount at all times. The British Society of Dowsers has an excellent code of ethics that you can find on their website, and I recommend that you familiarise yourself with it: https://britishdowsers.org/code-of-ethics/

If your interests lie in dowsing for health issues, remember that you must never diagnose or offer medical advice unless you are a medical professional. Only doctors can legally make a diagnosis, and your dowsing consultation is not a substitute for proper medical treatment.

Closure

Once you have completed your dowsing task, bring yourself back to a place of stillness and pause to consider the effects of your work. Dowse to ensure that you have done everything that needs to be done. Has your work been effective? If your dowsing suggests that it hasn't, you can try running through stages three and four of the protocol again to attempt to bring balance to the situation.

Once you are happy that everything is complete, start your pendulum going in the minimise direction and repeat the visualisation of connecting with the Earth as described in Stage One. Visualise your energy field returning to balance and equilibrium. Give thanks to your Spirit Team and any other 'helpers' that you have been working with.

Lastly, it's recommended practice to complete your 'grounding' by having something to eat and/or drink. Nothing brings you back into the physical faster than feeding the body. Don't miss out this stage if you have to drive somewhere; you need to be fully grounded or you risk having an accident.

As an ongoing discipline of psychic hygiene, it's advisable to check yourself for any unwanted energetic attachments that you may have picked up from a dowsing task. Or ask another dowsing colleague to check you; this can easily be done remotely. On several occasions, I have done this for a colleague (at their request) without telling them precisely when I was going to do the clearing, and they have called me immediately afterwards to let me know that they had felt something happening. These energies may be subtle but that doesn't mean they are not real.

The protocol can be adapted to place similar protective 'bubbles' around objects – your keys, phone, laptop, car and so on - even properties like your home or office. Many people also create a dedicated space within their own property that becomes their personal sacred space for dowsing work. If your garden is large enough, you might consider building a small stone circle or labyrinth to serve such a purpose.

Chapter 6

Spirit of Place

> *Spirit of place! It is for this we travel, to surprise its subtlety; and where it is a strong and dominant angel, that place, seen once, abides entire in the memory with all its own accidents, its habits, its breath, its name.*
>
> *-- ALICE MEYNELL, The Spirit of Place*

What is it that makes a place feel 'special'? What is it that makes a structure a good place for spiritual working? What gives it that numinous quality that leads us to define a space as sacred? Of course, there are particular configurations of telluric energies that we dowse for, but sometimes even a place with no obvious dowsing signature seems to exude a greater presence that cannot easily be accounted for. There is just a feeling that it presents something special, that you have entered an area that is somehow different from the rest of the world. Let's imagine that you are in a completely dark cave passage, and you are feeling your way along the walls, when suddenly you enter a large chamber. Even though you cannot see anything, there is some subtle quality in the atmosphere – maybe a noticeable change in the background acoustic, or air temperature, for example - that informs you that something has changed. Spirit of place is a bit like that. You know that you have crossed some *liminal* boundary.

Liminality (from the Latin *limen*, meaning 'a threshold') denotes a state that is betwixt or between, a transition, border or threshold between different states of being, places or times. It is the middle ground between one thing and another, a place of limbo having qualities of both but being identified with neither. A liminal place has more likelihood of hosting a supernatural event, or it can provide the optimum conditions for an act of magic to propagate successfully, especially if the act is performed at a liminal time. Examples of liminal places include caves, bogs, springs, rivers, coastlines, fords, marshes, passes, mountaintops and, importantly, boundaries. Liminality is a *boundary condition*.

If you have ever stood on a peat bog gazing into the mirrored blackness of a watery pool, you will understand the concept of liminality. The pull is strong, and the urge to throw oneself into the inky darkness can be hard to resist. Liminal boundaries seem to exude this sort of attraction, particularly those involving the four Classical elements. Consider the subconscious urge to throw oneself off a cliff edge or a high bridge, to dive into the sea from a moving ship, to explore the depths of a cave, or the simple fascination of staring into a fire – these are all examples of liminal effects. We are connecting with the s*piritus mundi* – the collective spirit of the world at these moments. Consciously, we are barely aware of it – that's why we use the term *subliminal* for these kinds of stimuli, influences that are below our normal threshold of awareness.

Caves are a good example of liminal places, for they are a transitional zone extending into the Underworld itself, the very womb of the Goddess. It is no surprise that the Neolithic shamans painted their ochre figures on the deepest cave walls to communicate with the Ancestors and the spirits of the animals they hunted. It is easy to picture the paintings coming to life and spirits emerging from the rock face in the flickering torchlight.

Undoubtedly, the best such cave that I have ever visited is the *Grotte de Niaux* in south-west France. The paintings, mostly of horses and bison, may not be as good as the better-known Lascaux caverns, but the experience of getting to them more than compensates. Tours must be booked in advance, and groups of 12 people at a time are guided over one kilometre into the darkness of the mountain with only a couple of flashlights to illuminate the journey. Talk about atmospheric! The children in the group were absolutely silent the whole way, no doubt expecting some giant or dragon to leap out at any moment (actually the returning tour group did play to this by making loud moaning and booming noises as they approached us but were still out of sight in the next chamber). When you finally get to the paintings, the atmosphere is almost tangible, and you have no doubt that you are in the presence of the Ancestors.

It is primarily these kinds of subliminal influences that will define the spirit of place for us, but of course there are many other components, including those invisible psychogeographic layers of folklore, art, history, and/or belief that combine with physical aspects such as vistas, simulacra, pathways, distinctive trees or rocks, and so forth. These all produce what the Romans called *genius loci*, the protective 'spirit of place', which was frequently personified in Roman times as a snake

Figure 13: Roman altar dedicated to the genius loci.

(which may refer to the serpentine flows of earth energy that are frequently detected at such places). At Auchendavy Roman fort on the Antonine Wall just outside Glasgow, five altars were found, one of which bears the inscription, 'GENIO TERRAE BRITTANICAE', translated as 'To the Spirit of the Land of Britain'. The remainder of the inscription gives the name Marcus Cocceius Firmus, a Centurion of the Second Legion Augustan (Fig. 13).[1]

In contemporary usage, the term *genius loci* refers to a location's distinctive atmosphere rather than necessarily a guardian spirit. However, in our shamanic dowsing worldview, the spirit of place can manifest in a variety of guises which can be located and identified through dowsing. It is possible to establish a creative dialogue with the spirit of place and, with its assistance, our strongly focused thoughts and healing intent can influence and repattern the etheric field in a gentle and respectful manner. The gardens of the Findhorn Community are a notable example of what can be achieved by working in co-operation with the spirit of place, but there are many other examples where the health and fecundity of the land has been greatly enhanced by people working sympathetically with the genius loci.

There may be an obvious focus for the spirit of place in the location you are working. It may be a particularly magnificent and unusual tree or bush, a strange rock formation, or a cave entrance perhaps. If there is no obvious focus for your attention, you can use your L-rods to direct you towards the spirit of place. Your rods may take you to some otherwise undistinguished and perfectly ordinary-looking patch of ground. This will most likely be an earth energy conflux such as a blind spring or power centre that you can check with your dowsing tool.

Communicating with the spirit of place is a meditative process. Go through the dowsing protocol, making sure that you are grounded and protected. Working from your heart centre, expand your energy field, imagining that you are placing a protective dome of light over the area of your work. Keep checking with your pendulum as you go through the process. Have it swinging in the search position, ensuring that it gives you a 'yes' response at each step. If it does not, stop and regroup, asking further questions to establish the problem.

Close your eyes and try to imagine what the spirit of place looks like. You may receive images, thoughts, emotions, sounds or even smells that indicate its presence. It can even be something as simple as a gust of wind or the rustle of leaves in the trees. These manifestations can be a very individual experience. The cry of a raven is a common manifestation for me, as the raven is my spirit animal. You might mentally visualise the genius loci as some non-physical being such as an angel, deva, a nature spirit, an elemental, dragon, or some other intelligent or quasi-intelligent being. It could even be a discarnate human site guardian (or guardians), there to protect the site from unwarranted interference. All these beings are powerful and deserve your respect.

It is important to be as clear as possible in your working with the spirit of place. Even if you have no clear image of it, you should still proceed as if there was one present. Be respectful of the space and do not proceed if there are obvious signs to the contrary – even if it is just a feeling that something isn't quite right. With your pendulum, dowse through some questions to establish what it is that you are dealing with – is it a flower, tree, or other form of deva? A site guardian? An elemental being? Is it welcoming? If so, respond with love, kindness, and respect. You wish to work co-operatively with this being, but does it wish to work with you? If you sense any darkness or hostility, withdraw from the area and reinforce your protection. Maybe you are not connecting with the genius loci, but something else? For instance, if a site has been abused or desecrated, there may be trapped discarnates or hostile entities who may not appreciate your presence. Here, you should work from a distance to try and appease them and, if you are capable, work with your spirit guides to remove the cause of the problem and bring healing to the space.

Cultural associations can also enhance the spirit of place, particularly if it is associated with local folk traditions or customs. At many sacred wells, the tradition of hanging a piece of cloth or 'cloot' on trees adjacent to the well to bring about healing of illness or other ailment is a popular piece of sympathetic magic dating back centuries. The tradition is that the affected body part is wrapped with the piece of cloth, which is then hung from a branch. As the cloth deteriorates and rots away, so the illness or ailment departs the sick person. In some traditions, sick children would be left by the well overnight in the hope that they would be cured, an act which gave rise to stories of the fairy folk leaving a 'changeling' child in place of the sick one.

Unfortunately, these days, the items used as rag offerings tend to be synthetic materials that don't disintegrate as quickly, with the result that most 'clootie wells' have trees groaning under the weight of fabric and struggling to survive. People also leave other offerings – I have seen whole T-shirts and other clothing items, shoes, photographs in plastic sleeves, Masonic aprons, tins, glass jars, candles, jewellery, crystals, cuddly toys, even plastic bags full of mementoes that may have held meaning to whoever left it, but to everyone else is just junk. Another widespread practice is to throw coins into the waters of the well, or even hammer them into the trunk of the clootie tree, which will eventually result in its death. It is both ironic and disturbing that the very rituals that are supposed to bring healing actually end up destroying the agency of that healing. Sadly, coming across this sort of litter has an adverse effect on subsequent visitors to the site as it detracts from the spirit of place instead of enhancing it, and rubbish like this can also be dangerous to local wildlife. Leave the area with nothing but positive intent and perhaps a small offering of some kind. Tobacco or cornmeal is traditional in First Nations teachings; some sage is also good, or you could leave some small biodegradable offering such as an oatcake or flower essence. Offerings should be eco-friendly and not noticeable by subsequent visitors. Leave the site as you would wish others to find it and take your rubbish home with you.

There may be other folklore traditions and legends associated with the locale that will help to build your mental picture of the spirit of place. Tales of ghosts, dragons, strange animal sightings, time distortions, saints, mythical beings (such as the Loch Ness monster) and so on, all contribute to the psychogeography of the area and provide valuable insights that will positively influence your interaction with the place. We can often gain insights into subtler aspects of the larger landscape by studying sites on a map and deriving connections between them. Some surprising relationships can turn up. I always plot my dowsing clients on Google Earth, which allows me to easily see interesting groupings and alignments that give insight into the landscape, such as clusters of cases around major motorways, railways, rivers, or geological faults. These in turn can provide clues as to the location of suitable nodal points for engaging with the larger landscape. To close this chapter, I offer two examples of such engagement; the first demonstrating the sort of information one can glean from studying cultural associations and folklore, the second about directly engaging with the genius loci of an area.

The Laidley Worm

The folklore ballad *The Laidley Worm of Spindlestone Heugh* is about a dragon associated with Bamburgh Castle ('laidley' or 'laidly' means 'loathsome'). The story tells of a king whose second marriage was to an evil and cold-hearted sorceress, who so disliked the king's daughter Princess Margaret that she turned her into a fearful dragon. The 'worm' was chased out of the castle and took refuge in a shallow cave at Spindlestone Heugh, a whinstone outcropping a few miles to the west, where it laid waste to the countryside in a seven-mile radius, devouring everything it came across. Local people consulted a mighty warlock in the area, who told them that the beast could only be appeased by being fed with the milk from seven cattle brought to it daily at sunset and poured into a trough at the foot of the Spindlestone, a natural rock column on the whinstone escarpment that the dragon liked to coil around (the site is still marked as 'Laidley Worm's Trough' on maps).

For seven miles east and seven miles west,
And seven miles north and south,
No blade of grass or corn would grow,
So deadly was her mouth.
The milk of seven streakit cows,
It was their cost to keep;
They brought her daily which she drank
Before she went to sleep.
At this day might be seen the cave
Where she lay faulded up,
And the trough o' stone the very same
Out of which she supped.

News of the dragon spread widely, eventually reaching the ears of Margaret's brother, the Prince known as 'The Childe Wynd', who was abroad on a long sea voyage. He immediately set sail to return to Bamburgh 'with three-and-thirty men', prepared to kill the worm and take his revenge on the evil Queen. But she raised a terrible storm at sea as he approached Bamburgh, forcing him to sail his ship into Budle Bay to the north of the castle, where the dragon lay in wait on the clifftops. Leaping ashore, the Prince raised his sword to strike down the fearsome worm, but at that point he heard his sister's voice whispering in his ear, insisting that he must stay his sword and instead kiss the dragon three times 'before the sun has set' to release the enchantment. Overcoming his revulsion, he did so, landing the final kiss just as the sun was setting, whereupon the dragon transformed back into his dear sister Meg.

> *O' quit thy sword, unbend thy brow,*
> *And give me kisses three;*
> *For though I am a poisonous worm,*
> *No hurt I'll do to thee.*
> *O' quit thy sword, unbend thy brow,*
> *And give me kisses three;*
> *If I'm not won ere the sun goes down,*
> *Won shall I never be. So,*
> *He quitted his sword and smoothed his brow,*
> *And gave her kisses three;*
> *She crept into the hole a worm,*
> *And came out a fayre ladye.*

Returning to the castle with a wand of protective rowan wood formed from the keel of his ship, the reunited siblings confronted the evil stepmother, turning her magic back upon herself and transforming her into a large venomous toad, which they chased into the well of the castle keep where it is said to reside to this day.

Interpretation

There are a number of clues in this folk tale that suggests it may contain some geomantic truths worthy of further exploration. The first clue, of course, is the mention of a dragon. As we know, dragons are frequently used as metaphor for the serpentine flows of telluric energies. Looking at a map of the area, it is clear that Spindlestone Heugh escarpment is a geological fault line, so one might expect strong earth energy manifestations and possibly even minor earthquakes around the area.

That the feeding of the Laidley Worm had to take place at sunset suggests that there may be a solar alignment involved. On studying the map, I discovered that there is a tiny island off the coast, one of the Farne Islands, with the name of 'Megstone'. I can't find any connection with the Princess Margaret of the story, but it seemed likely that there is some relation given the use of the diminutive name. The Farne Islands are the easternmost outcrop of the same whinstone ridge of the Spindlestone, so they are connected by the 'dragon' of the geological fault line. Furthermore, an alignment drawn from Megstone through the rock pillar of the Spindlestone runs over Chattonpark Hill, a Neolithic settlement with an extensive collection of cup and ring-marked stones, and on to Windy Gyle, a 619m peak lying on the border between England and Scotland with a Bronze Age burial cairn and a fallen standing stone called 'Split the De'il' (Devil) on its summit (Fig. 14).

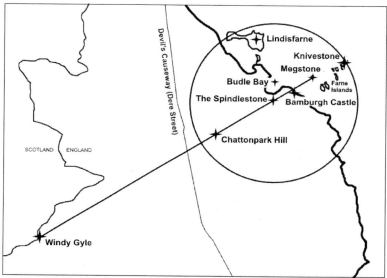

Figure 14: Principal sites and alignment to Windy Gyle

This alignment has an azimuth of 239 degrees, which is the direction of the Imbolc (and Samhain) *sunset* at this latitude (Fig. 15). This is the astronomical information that is encoded in the tale and explains why the sunset plays a significant part in the story. Of course, it is also entirely possible that the reverse alignment was of interest to the ancient peoples living in the settlement on Chattonpark Hill. I haven't checked this, but if the Spindlestone is visible from Chattonpark Hill, it should mark the position of the rising sun at Beltane and Lughnasadh (May 1/ Aug 1). The cup and ring marks may have been carved to record this solar alignment.

The feeding of the dragon with milk from seven cows is suggestive of a link to the goddess Bride or Brigid, whose sacred animal is the cow, and whose feast day is February 1st or Imbolc, one of the eight festivals of the Celtic year. Perhaps the seven in the text alludes to the remaining festivals? Seven of course could also represent the number of days in the week, but in either case some calendrical significance seems implied.

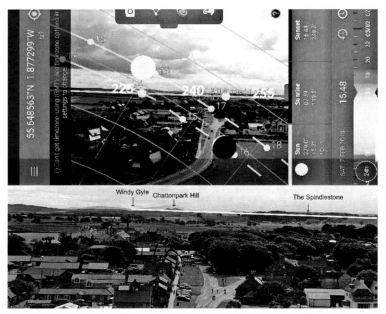

Figure 15: Imbolc sunset alignment using 'Sun Surveyor' app (top). Note: to get an overview of the landscape, I took these pictures from the castle ramparts, which is some distance south of the actual alignment.

The name Imbolc may derive from a Proto-European word meaning both 'milk' and 'cleansing', although it is most commonly thought to derive from 'ewe's milk', indicating the start of the lambing season.[2] Actually, many folklore tales of dragons seem to involve placating them milk; in another Northumbrian tale, the Lambton Worm has to be fed daily with the milk from *nine* cows. This idea probably descends from earlier folklore tales about serpents suckling on cows, an association that dates back at least as far as Roman times.

Then we have the occurrence of sacred numbers in the text, in particular the number seven and the number 33 in the 'three and thirty' men that Childe Wynd brought as his crew. 33 is considered a 'Master Number' (along with 11 and 22) in numerological circles, and has many correspondences, not least being the 33 degrees of Scottish Rite Freemasonry. It can be considered to represent an enlightened or 'perfected' state of being.

The number seven has sacred and mystical associations by the bucketload across all cultures. In sacred geometry, it is known as 'the virgin', because it cannot be divided by any number less than seven and produces no other number by multiplication within the first *dekad* of ten numbers. A 7-sided regular polygon, or heptagon, is the only figure that cannot be precisely produced using the traditional geometer's tools of straightedge and compasses; we can only attain a close approximation of the form.

> *A 7-sided figure is impossible to draw*
> *With perfect mathematical precision;*
> *And if you try to do it you are absolutely sure*
> *To find your efforts treated with derision.*
> *And yet there are philosophers who readily declare*
> *That nothing in this world is really true,*
> *And so I've drawn a heptagon by triangle and square,*
> *For any human purpose it will do.*
> * - JOHN MICHELL*

It is also tempting to interpret the seven as referring to energy centres or chakras in the manner of Peter Dawkins' and Gatekeeper Trust's 'Zoence' system. Peter defines a 'landscape temple' as an area possessing, "...an integral geomantic energy system with a complete set of chakras and auric field",[3] and much of his work involves pilgrimage through these landscapes. This analogy works rather well in this instance if we consider the Laidley Worm, coiled around the Spindlestone, as a metaphor for the kundalini energy that lies coiled like a serpent at the base of the spine. However, imposing this Eastern mystical system on such an alignment is an entirely modern conceit and I don't feel that it is necessary to anthropomorphise the ley in this way. However, it is an interesting analogy and Peter's system can certainly be a valid way to engage with a landscape.

There are other 'worm' tales associated with the north-east of England, such as the Lambton Worm of Wearside, the Linton Worm of the Scottish Borders (of which more in a moment), and the Sockburn Worm of the Tees valley, which has links with Durham Cathedral and is thought to be the inspiration for Lewis Carroll's *Jabberwocky*. Some historians speculate that these dragon stories allude to the serpent-like meandering explorations of an invading army unfamiliar with the territory, which in this area almost certainly refers to Viking raiders in their dragon-prowed longships. This seems a little simplistic to me, but if we accept this idea of a Viking origin for the story, perhaps the Laidley Worm tale is a distorted folk memory preserving some encoded information used by Viking navigators? A radius of seven miles around the Spindlestone encompasses the Holy Isle of Lindisfarne and also Knivestone, which is the outermost of the Farne Islands and the most hazardous to shipping. Conceivably, sighting for this alignment enabled them to avoid the treacherous Knivestone and the other Farne Islands and safely land their ships in the sheltered waters of Budle Bay.

However, returning to our geomantic interpretation where the dragons represent earth energy flows; Gary Biltcliffe and

Caroline Hoare have tracked a long-distance ley alignment running from the Farne Islands, through Bamburgh and on to Iona, which they call the 'Holy Axis'. As with other long-distance leys, this one carries associated male and female dragon currents that weave around the alignment. The first node point (where both currents cross) on land is in the well in the keep of Bamburgh Castle – the abode of the erstwhile Queen-turned-toad. Frogs and toads have several magical associations in folklore – is this some folk memory of the nodal power centre here? The male dragon current then continues on to pass through the Spindlestone itself on its way towards Scotland, while the female dragon current, after detouring northwards through Lindisfarne castle and priory, swings southwards again to cross the border at Kirk Yetholm and Linton, home of the aforementioned Linton Worm.[4]

So, what are we to make of this tangled web of dragon lore? Is it simply a folk memory of Viking invasions in the area? Or does it record some geomantic knowledge of the landscape, enabling effective land management techniques, perhaps to enhance crop fertility? I tend towards the latter explanation, but either way, there is undoubtedly more in the story that could yet be unravelled. 'The Childe Wynd' for example, may seem a rather portentous name for the Prince, but 'Childe' is an Old English term for a young nobleman who has not yet attained knighthood. 'Wynd' in this context could mean 'wind' and refer to some aspect of weather lore, perhaps a particular wind that the Viking navigators could seek out to enable them to safely plot a course into Budle Bay. Yet in Old Scots, 'wynd' means 'a narrow lane', which could be an oblique reference to the ley alignment marking the distant Windy Gyle. 'Gyle' is thought to be a Northumbrian word meaning 'a hollow passage between hills', which seems appropriate in this context.[5] The 'Split the De'il' stone on the summit definitely sounds like a visual sightline marker, and the ley running to Windy Gyle 'splits' the skyline between The Cheviot and Hedgehope Hill (the 'hollow passage'?). It could also be said to split the 'Devil's Causeway', the name given to the Roman Road of Dere Street, which crosses the alignment almost exactly halfway along its length at roughly 13 miles from both Windy Gyle and Megstone.

Many of these interpretations may seem highly speculative, yet they provide meaning and context to the landscape that is useful to the practising geomancer by creating an intricate psychogeographic tapestry that highlights several nodal points where connection with the *genius loci*, or Spirit of Place is enhanced. This allows dowsing and geomantic techniques to be profitably applied towards the healing and revitalisation of the land. By approaching the wider landscape in this way, the geomancer becomes psychically connected to the area, enhancing their ability to initiate change on a more localised level.[6]

Zen Tea in BC

The Earth has music for those who would listen, as the saying goes, and sometimes the landscape speaks to you directly, as it did in this tale of a landscape healing exercise that I performed with some members of the Canadian Society of Questers, following my presentation at their 2012 conference in Harrison Hot Springs, British Columbia.

After the conference, organiser Merlin Beltain arranged for me to deliver some talks and workshops to local dowsing chapters in the Vernon, BC area. So it was that I found myself one morning in the company of Questers Joan, Kim and Jesse, standing at a hilltop viewpoint between Vernon and Coldstream, looking eastwards up the valley, where the group thought that there was some sort of energy blockage.

Merlin explained that they had worked on the area some years before with Vancouver-based geomancer Dieter Bay, a protégé of Marko Pogacnik. Dieter had identified the main energy 'fountain' and 'sink' zones and they had cleared and re-established energy flows between these; however, the group felt that there was still a blockage of energy over this particular valley that needed resolved. Merlin told us of experiencing some dreams where she had visions of 'Jabba the Hutt' from Star Wars sitting athwart the blocked energy line and laughing at her.

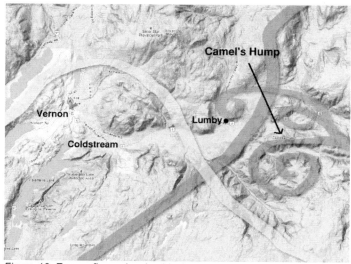

Figure 16: Energy flows showing blockage

"What, you mean like that hill at the end of the valley?" I asked, pointing at the distinctive 'Camel's Hump' hill in the distance. The resemblance to Jabba the Hutt was immediately obvious to everyone. It was clear that this was the source of the disruption (Fig. 16). Two more energy lines flowed to the northwest and southwest, crossing the valley and running behind the hills at each side. Between, where there should have been a flow running along the valley towards us, the land appeared to be in deep shadow.

Merlin left us, having other business to attend to and so, after establishing where we needed to work and ensuring that we had permission from our highest ideals to work with the landscape, the rest of us set off in the car and drove towards the Camel's Hump.

As we drove, we were tuning in with our pendulums and asking the land and our spirit teams for guidance on where we needed to be. Some miles east, as we entered the town of Lumby, both Joan and I got strong reactions from our pendulums. I felt like there was a tautness or contraction about the energies in the town, and Joan said she felt short of breath. This appeared to be the blockage that we were seeking. We drove onwards through the town and turned off onto a side road leading towards the Camel's Hump, and hadn't gone very far before my pendulum indicated that we had reached a suitable spot for working, which was on a bridge over a small creek that ran back in the direction of Lumby. Here, it dowsed as most appropriate to work with the energy of the water, which would hopefully carry our healing intention towards the town. Standing on the bridge, we asked permission to work, invoked the local spirit of place, and asked for unconditional love and healing energy for the highest good of all beings to be sent downstream to release the energy blockage in Lumby. As we finished sending energy, I made some offerings of flower essences to the waters and, having checked that we had nothing more to do, set off back to town.

On the eastern outskirts of town, we found a spot where three creeks join, including the one we had worked on. This felt like it should be a key node to work with the three dragon flows of the valley, therefore we parked the car and dowsed for the best place from which to work. We were unable to get to the exact spot where all three creeks merged, but dowsing led us to a spot just upstream of this alongside 'our' creek, between the town and a grim-looking industrial estate with a view of the Camel's Hump behind.

Here we joined hands and made a circle, tuned in to the local spirit of place, and began dowsing again to check that our 'upstream' working had been effective. We all felt that the industrial estate had some part to play in the energy blockage and that some further work would be beneficial here. Joan and I were both using our pendulums to gauge the energy as we worked and were deeply engaged with the process. Suddenly I heard Joan exclaim "Oh!", and at the same moment my pendulum *instantly* reversed direction. Surprised, I looked up to see Kim spreading what looked like the contents of a tea bag across our path. This turned out to be a blend called Zen tea, and it appeared to have instantaneously transformed the detrimental energies and released the blockage! Further dowsing checks confirmed this, and also that our work was finished. Excited, we stopped in the centre of Lumby for a final check and found that the whole place felt much clearer and more welcoming (Fig. 17). Job done!

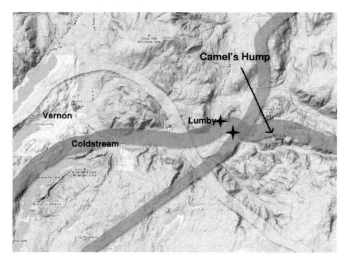

Figure 17: Restored energy flow. The stars mark the two locations worked on.

Of course, the Zen tea was not the transformative agent in itself, but an elemental aid to the intention of the practitioner. Kim could have used a vibrational essence, beaten a gong or drum, chanted or whatever else felt appropriate at the time. The interesting point is that it had clearly triggered the healing release that both Joan and I simultaneously detected.[7]

Chapter 7
Practitioner's Guide

> *It isn't that the world of appearance is wrong; it isn't that there aren't objects out here, at one level of reality. It's that if you penetrate through and look at the universe with a holographic system you arrive a different view, a different reality. And that other reality can explain things that have hitherto remained inexplicable scientifically: paranormal phenomena, synchronicities, the apparently meaningful coincidence of events.*
>
> *-- KARL PRIBRAM*

In approaching a space that you want to work with, particularly a traumatised space carrying geopathic stress, it can sometimes be difficult to ascertain precisely where the problem lies. You wish to 'tune in' to the specific aspect that you need to dowse, but, like an onion, there can be many energetic layers to sort through before you find the one holding the trauma. There may be more than one level requiring attention and you may need to work through these in ordered sequence. Generally, one has to first consider the history of the area. In the UK and Europe in particular, the many historical layers overlaying the landscape often muddy the waters considerably. The range of historical trauma could be anything from the present day back through two World Wars, the Middle Ages, the Crusades, Anglo-Saxons, Vikings, Roman Empire and so on, extending right back to the Neolithic in many areas. Pinpointing the time zone that the trauma dates from can take some time and is a test of your dowsing ability. This is less of an issue in places like North America, where you basically have early settlers, before immediately connecting with a layer of First Nations energy. I certainly find it easier to get right to the heart of the issue when working in North America.

These historical residues are sometimes called 'remanence' by dowsers, although the term is more commonly applied to the energetic signature from an artefact that has lain in place for some time. For instance, a long-decayed wooden post will leave a chemical residue in the soil that a good archaeological dowser may be able to detect. Remanence can also refer to obfuscating energy patterns left behind by previous dowsers, either intentionally or unintentionally.[1]

Your intuition is the best key to unravelling these various layers, and if you have worked to cultivate sensitivity with your dowsing, it will often be immediately obvious to you what the main issue is when you are on-site. Sometimes however, you may need a 'map of the territory' to help you categorise your findings and, hopefully, this chapter will help you to develop your own.

Geology

I usually start by researching the geology of the area. It's always worth doing some research on the local geology, as this will affect water flows in the landscape and the general 'feel' of the land. I think that a dowser is most effective when working on the same sort of geology that he or she was born on – in my case this was sandstone and coal. It's hard to describe how this affects my dowsing, but (for example) when I'm working on places with a clay substrate, my dowsing feels a little bit sluggish, and places where the geology is largely chalk (like the South Downs in England) feel somehow bland. When tuning in to the site in chalky areas, I find it helpful to focus on the outcrops of flint within the chalk. Flint is a sedimentary cryptocrystalline form of quartz,[2] and, like quartz, can be useful in the diversion and manipulation of energy lines. I have successfully diverted energy lines within homes using a couple of large lumps of flint. Terry Pratchett demonstrates his knowledge of this in the Tiffany Aching stories, when Granny Weatherwax says, "*The* bones *of the hills is flint. It's hard and sharp and useful. King of stones.*"[3]

It's certainly worth considering the effects of different geologies when doing your initial research, as a 'livelier' geology will affect the intensity of any dowseable manifestations. Igneous bedrocks like granite, which contains a lot of quartz, are going to be more energetic than places with a largely sedimentary geology. Volcanic regions will be more energetic than deserts, mountainous areas more energetic than flood plains, and so on. You can often research local geology using online sources. In the UK, there is an excellent interactive mapping service provided by the British Geological Survey (BGS).[4] In the States, the USGS website has similar facilities.[5]

For practice, I invite you to try dowsing the energy levels of some geology for yourself for each of the places listed in the table below. Using a simple 1-10 pendulum chart, or just counting from 1 to 10 until your pendulum reacts, mentally picture yourself in the following areas and dowse to see how they feel to you. It doesn't matter whether you have actually visited the area or not, you can still connect with them through your dowsing tool, and this exercise is just for fun. Look each area up in Google Maps if you feel that you need a better connection. Afterwards, look up each place using the previously mentioned online geological references to see if you find any correspondence with what you have dowsed.

Location	Energy (1-10)	Location	Energy (1-10)
Where you are right now		Aberdeen, Scotland	
The place you were born		Sahara Desert	
New York City		London, England	
Glastonbury Tor, England		Mt Fuji, Japan	
Iona, Scotland		Great Salt Lake, Utah	
Alice Springs, Australia		The South Pole	

How did that work out for you? Were there any unexpected results? Generally, you would expect the geology to reflect your dowsing result, so that places with igneous or metamorphic geology will be more energetic than places with sedimentary-type geology. But perhaps there is some other aspect of the area that affected your dowsing result? Here's where some further research into the area's geology might turn up some insights.

Having covered the physical conditions, let's move on to the metaphysical side of the picture – the area which many people find challenging to accept the reality of their findings, perhaps because their worldview does not admit the possibility that beings like ghosts, demons or aliens actually exist in any objective form. As I mentioned in Chapter 4, belief is not necessary to work within this terminology. Just accept what you are reading 'as if' it is objectively real. Think of a cake recipe with yourself as the chef who has to bake it all together.

Earth Energies (Energetic Anatomy)

In this category, we are still dealing mostly with naturally occurring phenomena, although some of these can also be affected, or even created in some cases, by human activity.

1. **Yin chi paths.** As we have learned, the energy of water flowing naturally in the earth is of a *yin*, or receptive, nature. We are *yang* in relation to yin chi, and it has a draining effect on the human aura, so sleeping over a water line is regarded as detrimental, compromising the immune system and leading to geopathic stress. We can quantify the intensity of the geopathic stress by either using a pendulum chart, or by counting percentages ("Is it more than..." etc.). Many dowsers use a 0 – 16 scale known as the von Pohl scale (after its originator) to measure the strength of geopathic stress, in which 0 represents the healthy 7.83 Schumann frequency, and levels of 9 and above are regarded as dangerous to human life. We also need to know how many water lines are affecting the property, and whether they are from a blind spring (dome) or downshaft, as these have different energetic signatures. If the offending water lines come from a blind spring, you can work on the one feeding the spring, which will heal the entire system at once.

2. **Yang chi paths.** Most energy leys and serpentine energy lines are considered yang, masculine or active in nature. We are yin in relation to them, so they will give energy to us. These yang energies are actively sought out for sites of churches, temples, and other sacred spaces, and in certain circumstances, they can also be beneficial in the home. Yet while it might be a positive benefit to have an energy ley running through your meditation room or your workspace, it is not beneficial to have one running through your bed as it

will interfere with sleep. Energy leys can become stressed and out of balance and, because of their higher informational content, tend to be carriers of spirit activity. I usually dowse the state of these using a plus/minus percentage chart. You may wish to include other lines (such as spirit pathways) in this category.

3. **Carrier Matrices (Grids).** Can be yin or yang in nature. Hartmann, Curry, Benker and similar earth grids are believed to be natural earth energy fields related to geomagnetic activity, although their interpretation can vary between dowsers. I find that grid lines become bunched up in the presence of geopathic stress, so they are a good secondary indicator of its presence. Double-strength grid crossing points will produce vortices, and these are likely to be detrimental if they occur inside the property. I don't usually worry too much about grids unless a grid problem is indicated on my pre-visit checklist, in which case I will dowse for them on site. Perhaps there is a crossing of double-strength negative or positive lines that is creating a vortex, or perhaps there is some other interaction between a grid and another geopathic source like a water line or stressed energy ley that you need to work with. Unless they require urgent attention, most grid disturbances will resolve themselves over a short period once you have carried out the remedial work on the water and energetic systems. It is also possible to find geometric grids conforming to the layout of buildings, for example churches or cathedrals utilising the principles of sacred geometry in their construction. These may overlay, distort, or even completely suppress the natural earth grids. In some cases, conscious intention may manipulate grids. The Hartmann grid, in particular, is often found to be absent from many temples and other sacred spaces.[6]

4. **Psychic Membranes or Boundaries.** These are commonly found in buildings that have undergone some renovation, or where a newer structure has been built on the site of an older building. Over time, buildings develop their own etheric signature, which becomes reinforced in accordance with the amount and type of human activity within. Thus, sacred buildings where there is frequent ceremony have a very well-developed psychic boundary, regularly reinforced with positive intention, that reflects their position in the community landscape whilst offering protection to the sacred atmosphere within. Of course, the opposite is also true, so institutional buildings such as hospitals, asylums or prisons will project a boundary that is more chaotic, although it can be equally strong in some cases. When a building is removed, this energetic signature remains in the landscape and will affect future structures on the site – this is why it is important to decommission a church when it is no longer in use. A strong psychic membrane also acts as a protective filter, keeping out undesirable energies. When a building is extended or the internal layout is altered, you will be able to dowse this psychic boundary where a door or wall used to be, and energetic issues are frequently found in houses with conservatory extensions, as the new part is outside of the original boundary. In such cases, the dowser can mentally 're-draw' the new boundary using focused intent. It is also possible to place a psychic boundary around objects and places, as the numerous 'beating the bounds' or 'riding the Marches' traditions that still take place today in many towns and villages attest.

5. **Interdimensional Portals.** Although these do occur naturally, in a secular situation they are usually the result of some human activity, either intentional or unintentional.

Natural portals can be found at particularly strong nexus of earth energies such as the intersection of several major energy leys or dragon lines, vortex zones and gravitational anomalies (like the many 'mystery spot' attractions found in North America) and so on. Human-created portals may be deliberately crafted gateways that are regularly maintained, such as those within a church. They can also form as a result of heavy alcohol or drug use (particularly psychoactive drugs) or poorly controlled practice arising from magickal rituals, spiritualist seances, or Ouija board sessions. Religious institutions like churches and cathedrals will have open portals built into the etheric structure; indeed, it is essential to have these for the building to function as it should. However, it is less desirable to have open portals in a secular or domestic situation as usually the human inhabitants have little or no control over what may come through the gateway. Typical portal activity includes glowing balls of light (orbs), odd creatures, strange shapes, unexplained mists or fog and unusual sounds. Portals may also very in intensity, size, or other quality, with the lunar and solar cycles. Inappropriate portals can be closed using focused intent by mentally drawing the sides together then sealing it with a visualised symbol like a cross or pentagram. You can also ask Archangel Michael to help with his flaming sword. Always check for the presence of guardians before you attempt to close a portal.

A colleague of mine, in the early days of her practice, lived on the edge of a housing estate that had been built on the site of an old monastery. Her pre-teen daughters complained of strange men in hoods and robes walking through their bedroom at night and, after some dowsing work, she determined that there was a portal on the upper floor that admitted a steady stream of ghostly monks at regular intervals. Despite the best efforts of several dowsers, she was unable to close this portal and eventually had to move to a new house.

Place Memory/ Predecessor Chi

There are two main components of predecessor chi that the practitioner needs to be aware of. *Place Memory* refers to the stories and cultural beliefs that become attached to a place over time – the oral history of the location if you will. Events, both mundane and exceptional, leave their imprint on the space: reconstructions, extensions, accidents, fires, and so on – all have effects on the atmosphere. This is an energetic stratum that is primarily a passive, human-held layer, distributed through the collective consciousness of the neighbourhood in snippets of information, gossip, legends and symbolism. A building with distinctive architectural features such as a Gothic mansion may evoke an aura of mystery and grandeur in its inhabitants, or equally could lead to spooky tales of ghosts and witches amongst local children. Civic buildings like council offices or theatres will have their own distinctive place memory based on their activity. Theatres are particularly strong in this regard because of the collective emotional plenitude resulting from years of audience engagement, and no self-respecting theatre is without its own resident ghost or two. A surprising number of theatres also have their stages built over underground water flows, which helps to energise the space.

Buildings that have been repurposed from their initial use can retain the place memory of their former self, and in some cases this can infuse the local landscape to such an extent that, even if the building has been demolished, homes subsequently built on the site are still affected by it. I've had a few clients in new build homes on the sites of former structures where there is clearly a lingering resonance from the previous building.

A client, whose house was built on the site of an old railway station, suffered from anxiety and poor sleep. She could not pinpoint the cause of the anxiety and could only tell me that she had a sense of something heavy and threatening approaching in the darkness. Some dowsing work and consulting of old maps of the area revealed that her bed was situated directly on the route of the former main rail line! Once this was established and the energy pattern neutralised with dowsing, the problem disappeared.

Predecessor Chi is another passively-held layer that relates to residue left behind from extreme psycho-spiritual events that have occurred in the space, for example the resonance from any deaths that have happened in the house, particularly traumatic deaths like suicides or murders. There are many historical instances where subsequent inhabitants of a house have experienced similar traumatic behaviour patterns manifesting in themselves, or the house may become plagued by poltergeist activity or other hauntings. Habitual drug use, particularly alcoholism, use of opioids or strong hallucinogens can leave such a stain on the house atmosphere. Typically, we will see similar behaviours manifesting in subsequent inhabitants of the house over time. I've seen a few houses that exhibit this, what we might call, 'serial alcoholism'. Discarnate humans who were alcoholics or drug addicts in life seek out this energy in others and gain energy from it, often inducing the same condition in those they draw their energy from. Before I learned how to maintain my own psychic protection, I used to feel uncomfortable going into pubs and bars for this reason (there is a reason why strong liquor is called 'spirits'...!).

Curses and Thoughtforms

There can be a more active psycho-emotional human-held layer that is created either intentionally or unintentionally by particular thought patterns. This can be a result of some dark magick such as a psychic attack, where the recipient may not even be aware of the root cause. It can also result from what we tend to inaccurately label *curses*.

To *curse* usually refers to 'a solemn utterance intended to invoke a supernatural power to inflict harm or punishment on someone or something',[7] and we think of a curse as an execration uttered by a witch or sorcerer against a person who has done them great wrong. Yet a curse doesn't have to be of the death-wish-pointing-bone type. The word 'curse' is highly emotionally charged and pejorative to use for something that can be as simple as an offhand insult uttered without thinking. How many times have you found yourself deeply offended or upset by a derogatory remark? How many times have you upset someone else in the same way? These are curses too, and such thought patterns may be carried for years, causing untold mental suffering in the recipient even though the progenitor may be blissfully unaware of its continued effect.

A *thoughtform* generally refers to a consciously created entity, which may appear to be quasi-intelligent and often results from magickal activity, like a witch's familiar for instance. But it can also simply be a residual energetic construct intentionally placed for some reason, which may be as innocent as a protection symbol on a doorway or object. There was a venerable member of the BSD, who shall remain nameless, known for phoning friends of an evening to ask, "I've just sent you a line – can you dowse it for me?" That's a thoughtform.

Power Objects

Something of a sub-category here, *power objects* are artefacts that contain an energetic signature and can be beneficial or detrimental. Typical power objects are things like tribal masks or ritual statuary brought home from foreign trips; but they could be any pieces of art, furniture, weapons, historical paraphernalia and suchlike. These may have been actively imprinted with the previous owner or maker's intent before finding their way to you, and that intent may be exerting an influence on you or your home. A power object could even be something as innocuous as an item of furniture unintentionally imprinted with a depressing aura that exudes from it, perhaps because its maker was miserable at the time of its construction, or maybe it was associated with some life trauma experienced by a former owner.

Spirit Consciousness

Broadly speaking, by *spirit consciousness* we are talking about intelligent or quasi-intelligent non-corporeal beings that it is possible to have a meaningful dialogue with using dowsing or shamanic methods. This category is by no means exhaustive and does not include the numerous non-intelligent energies that may be encountered.

Human discarnates

Human discarnates are what many people call ghosts, although there are other connotations to that word, so I prefer 'discarnates' to refer to the spirit or shade of someone who has died but not moved on. Discarnates can be earthbound for several reasons; perhaps they are unable to let go because they are emotionally attached to a loved one who is still incarnate, or equally the loved one remaining is so bereft at their loss that the spirit is unwilling or unable to leave. In situations of violent or accidental death, the discarnate may not actually realise that they have died, and in such cases the spirit requires a gentle reminder of the situation to enable them to depart. The discarnate spirit may be reluctant to move on through fear of the 'other side' if they had a strong religious belief system where they genuinely believe that they might be facing Judgement or going to Hell for some imagined transgressions in their lifetime. There may be some work that they have left incomplete and are reluctant to move on before they can communicate this to a living relative. For example, grandmother has died without telling her family that her life savings are buried under the floorboards or hasn't passed on the password details for her offshore account in the Cayman Islands. Sometimes the discarnate is just plain mischievous and will try to trick you into thinking that it has gone when it actually hasn't. These are often the trickiest ones to deal with and may require more than one attempt before they can be moved on.

Symptoms of an earthbound discarnate can include physical manifestations like slamming or opening doors or windows, half-heard voices or sounds, a strong feeling of presence, perhaps a particular scent or even touch. Sensitive people may occasionally see an apparition of the discarnate in some form. Contrary to what many people think, the most common hauntings are usually more connected with place memory than intelligent discarnates and, although often mistaken for such, are actually just a residual imprint on the etheric environment that replays like a tape recording under the right conditions. The 'grey ladies' and phantom footsteps that grace many stately homes generally form this type of haunting.

Guardian spirits

Another category of discarnate, that you are most likely to encounter at an ancient site, is a guardian spirit. Most often, these are human discarnates who are attached to a particular place and effectively become the genius loci for that site. There are many possible reasons for this – they may have become emotionally attached to the site during life and have voluntarily adopted a vow to look after it; they may have been some revered elder who has perhaps been cremated or buried at the site; they may even have been deliberately sacrificed to fulfil the function of guardian. These guardians are there to preserve the energy of the place and may take exception to anyone disturbing the site. Guardians are sometimes also encountered in connection with an interdimensional portal. Whatever their motivation, site guardians should be acknowledged and respected when encountered, and often they will impart information and maybe even a psychic gift for you if asked nicely. Usually site guardians are simply curious about what you are doing and, providing your intentions are good, may even be called upon to assist you in bringing balance to a space.

In extremely old properties, you may sometimes encounter animal guardian spirits, where an animal has been walled up within the space or buried beneath the threshold or hearth as an act of protection magick. Cats seem to be a favourite choice for this. Frequently these are discovered when new owners carry out modifications to the building and open up a wall. If proving problematic, they can be appeased by acknowledging their presence in some way, perhaps by designating a small space or ornament as their new home and making small offerings to them.

Non-human

1. **Elementals**. There are various orders of elemental beings, and not all are intelligent enough for us to be able to open a dialogue, but it's certainly possible to seek guidance from the four primary elementals of Earth, Air, Fire and Water – the gnomes, sylphs, salamanders and undines. Elemental disturbances tend to manifest as faults in the fabric of a building, such as drainage problems, bad smells, building cracks and subsidence and so on. Thus, a leaky cellar or persistent plumbing issues can indicate a water elemental disturbance; subsidence or problems with the fabric of the building suggest earth elemental problems; persistent inexplicable wiring issues can be air elemental imbalances and so on. As a general rule, elemental imbalances will affect the building systems on a fundamental level. Try to find out what the specific problem is and establish what needs done to rectify the situation. Do the elementals need some sort of offering or acknowledgement? Have you also replaced that worn tap washer? Fixed that mould problem? Reinforced that sagging basement wall? You need to resolve the physical issues as well as the spiritual.

2. **Spirit of place/ Nature Spirits**. Mythology has provided us with a vast panoply of nature spirits, which vary not only from country to country but even from region to region within countries. In Britain alone, we have terms like fairy, elf, pixie, brownie, boggart, redcap, sprite… to name just a few. Nature spirit problems are often related to elemental disturbances, but manifest at a higher resonance. They usually first appear as small, annoying gremlins or glitches – unexplained computer crashes, television interference, flickering lights, and other minor faults that are more irritating than actually damaging, and continue to occur for no apparent reason even when you have eliminated any more tangible cause. Indications of elf/faery activity may include sensations of being watched, a feeling that someone else is present, or an apprehensive sense that something is about to happen at any moment, as though a mischievous child was about to play a prank on you. Such disruptions can be common in new housing sites, a classic example being a former greenfield site where construction has left no natural corridors of vegetation connecting to it. Here, the problems will typically manifest in the last house to be built, as the nature spirits are displaced house by house until they have nowhere else to go. It's interesting to consider that the last house in the village is traditionally the one where the village witch lived, as witches were the only people who could deal with these problems! Displaced nature spirits can usually be placated and relocated to a more suitable nearby site.

3. **Landscape spirits/ Location specific devas** The term *deva* is a Sanskrit word, found in Vedic literature dating from the 2nd millennium BCE, which translates roughly as 'heavenly, divine, terrestrial things of high excellence, exalted, shining ones'.[8] They generally refer to some sort of

minor deity in both Hinduism and Buddhism traditions. In modern Western usage however, the term is applied as an alternative paradigm of locational consciousness governing all aspects of manifestation, from the smallest bud up to the planet itself and even beyond. Although there is clearly overlap with our concept of nature spirits at the vegetative level, it is useful to embrace a concept of devas responsible for larger areas such as the garden, neighbourhood, town, or country as a whole. It's always worthwhile to check in with the local devas as they have a wide awareness of trauma in the landscape under their control, and are essential collaborators in bringing healing to the landscape. Start by asking the most local deva for assistance, and if needed, work up to higher level devas of the garden, neighbourhood, or town.

4. **Animal spirits.** It is rare, but not unheard of, to encounter the spirit of a wild animal remaining earthbound after death. Domestic animals, particularly favoured family pets, do sometimes remain attached to the family and have trouble moving on. They may become distressed if the house has changed hands and the original family has moved. As previously mentioned, it is also possible to encounter animal guardian spirits in older buildings. Animal spirits may also be personal totem or power animals, usually encountered through meditation, dream work or shamanic journeying; these of course you will want to keep as part of your spirit team.

I once had a spirit pet dog return home with me after a consultation. He was very friendly, and I could sense him lying on the foot of the bed at night, so he wasn't causing trouble, but he was a little confused and missing his family. After a few weeks (and some dowsing dialogues) he went on of his own accord.

5. **Inter-dimensional beings (aliens etc.).** Often associated with open portals. Extra-terrestrial encounters seem to be more common these days, and there is some thought that they are simply the modern archetypes of traditional nature spirits, manifesting in a more contemporary fashion better suited to our modern consciousness. This idea has some traction, particularly when you compare tales of alien abduction with old stories of people being 'taken by the fairies' and disappearing, sometimes for years at a time. Modern concepts of fairies and nature spirits tend to portray them as small, friendly, benevolent beings, in stark contrast to older tales where they are large, aloof, and quite frightening at times, so it may be that the alien archetype has arisen to fill this niche. Because of their strangeness, they can induce fear and uncertainty when encountered. It's difficult to establish purpose or motive with aliens as they are completely amoral by human standards and we have no common frame of reference. Use your guides or Archangel Michael to get them to leave, then close the portal.

When I was much younger, and before I learned how to properly protect myself, I went through a period where I did not like sitting in a room with open curtains when it was dark outside, as

I had an irrational fear of alien heads appearing outside the window. This was just after I'd read Whitley Strieber's *Communion* book describing his abduction experiences, the one with a cover showing the head of a 'Grey' in closeup, which may have had something to do with it. The feeling lingered for some months. On one occasion, in that dreamlike half-awake state before falling asleep, I became aware of a group of Grey-like beings standing at the foot of the bed. Fortunately, they left after I mentally acknowledged their presence and asked them to leave.

6. Other beings. This is an overly broad category, and tends to swiftly expand to include a greater variety of beings once you start working in this area. But here are a few things to look out for.

a.   **Trolls** I place these in a separate category to nature spirits as they have a particular flavour of their own. Trolls are elemental water/earth beings that tend to keep away from people but have a very particular sense of psychic trespass on their territory. Originating in Scandinavian folklore, trolls are now well-ensconced in Western mindsets through the works of Tolkien and other authors, and films like the wonderful 2010 Norwegian 'mockumentary' movie *Trollhunter*. Troll energy is limited to a defined area (its 'territory'), and they don't like this being disturbed. A sudden sense of not wanting to go any farther along a gloomy path in a wood is a sign of troll presence, as is a general sense of heaviness about an area that lifts rapidly when you leave.

b. **Demons** Broadly speaking, demons are fear-based quasi-intelligent independent forces that we carry in our own energy field. They are capricious, masters of concealment and frequently of malevolent intent. Many cultures throughout history have concepts of demons. In the Western magickal tradition, demons are spirit beings who can be summoned to do the will of the magician, whereas in Christian theology demons are corrupted spirits who may be souls of the wicked deceased, or those fallen angels who were cast out of Heaven along with Lucifer. Contemporary Roman Catholicism holds that angels and demons are real beings and not symbolic devices, and that they can possess humans, resulting in the need for exorcism. The key phrase here is 'possess humans', and often the first sign of demonic activity is a change in the behaviour of the person affected. To sensitive people, demons sometimes display what looks like red glowing eyes in the energy field. There are some modern psychological practitioners who regard these manifestations as repressed personality fragments – 'shadow' aspects that we are not willing to consciously acknowledge; thus they are subsumed into our personal unconscious, or the 'Underworld' as discussed in Chapter 4. [9] Enclose the demon in a geometric cage of light, or use the 'Golden Net of Hephaestus' technique described at the end of this chapter to draw it out of the energy field where you can deal with it appropriately. Ask a suitable intermediary spirit such as Archangel Michael to relocate the demon to its proper place; don't try to do this yourself.

c. **Magickally-created entities** These result from sloppy or unethical magickal practice and may be deliberately created entities, such as familiars or self-sustaining thought-forms, or a host of other quasi-intelligent beings. Sometimes these can linger in place for many years if they have not been properly dismissed.

One of my early cases involved clearing a bedroom where both mother and daughter, when sleeping there independently, had woken in the night feeling a presence lying on top trying to have sex with them. In the parlance of Classical magick, such a spirit is called an incubus (the female version is a succubus). Dowsing determined that it had been in that location for a couple of hundred years, created from a magickal ritual and never dismissed. It took no small effort on my part to get rid of it, eventually invoking the help of all four Archangels of the Quarters to help. The next day, the mother called to tell me that they had been sitting outside on the patio having tea, when a single white feather – widely regarded as a sign of angelic communication - fell out of the sky and landed on the table between them. A good day-sign and a successful clearing!

d. **Incoherent or fragmented entities** A range of quasi-intelligent or non-intelligent beings exist that one may encounter, such as black, furry, spider-like things. In traditional Wiccan parlance, these are known as 'gronkydoddles' or 'gronkydoodles'. They are thought to be related to minor nature spirits like pixies but are mostly just amorphous lower astral debris that hasn't been cleaned up. Ask your gnomes to create a psychic rubbish heap then visualise wielding an imaginary vacuum cleaner removing the rubbish.

Spirit release

Spirit release is a whole discipline in itself and is not something that should be attempted by novices. It is a shamanic act that involves opening a portal and guiding the spirit to where it needs to go, and, although the procedure described here may sound simple, it is anything but and it's easy to make mistakes. First of all, you need to be in a secure and appropriately protected psychic space and connected with your spirit guides. It is recommended to do this work off-site if possible. Ask the discarnate to come and stand before you and strongly visualise that it does so. Open a portal by visualising a column of light surrounding the discarnate and ask one of your spirit guides to take the spirit to where they need to go. Do not try to take the spirit yourself as you may have trouble returning. You can also call upon the services of a psychopomp such as Hermes, Gabriel, or Anubis – all archetypes who traditionally help souls to cross over. I picture a sort of magic elevator rising up the column of light, carrying both the discarnate and the guide. Some discarnates require reassurance that it's all right for them to leave, which may require some gentle persuasion or even a white lie from you to get them to move. You will often receive a psychic image of other beings waiting in the light to welcome the discarnate, or some other confirmatory vision. During this process, keep your pendulum moving and ask your guide to let you know they have completed the task and returned by indicating a change in the pendulum motion. It does take practice to do this work successfully and it is best learned by working alongside a practitioner or group more experienced in the work, but it is a hugely compassionate act and is rewarding work to perform. For more information, look up the Spirit Release Forum online.[10] I also recommend Sue Allen's book *Spirit Release – a Practical Workbook*.

Non-human discarnates frequently just need gentle and apologetic relocation to a more suitable area. Try a psychopomp like Gabriel, Pan, or Gaia, or ask your guides for one. If you can't find a suitable intermediary, try asking for the being's mother (everything has a mother, right?).

Spirit healing and re-placement checklist

- Work from a place of compassion with unconditional love, in an appropriate psychic space.
- Be patient in the presence of fear. Fear is a sign that you are missing something. Pause and regroup.
- Use your spirit guides and other helpers for healing and psychopomp spirits for re-placement.
- Attend appropriately and in guided sequence to associated geopathic stress, place memory, residue patterns from cleared spirits, and psychic structure. As spirits and other psychic boojums draw their energy from yang pathways, in almost every case they should be dealt with before any geopathic stress work or they may decide to attach to the nearest alternative energy source, which is likely to be you or your client.

Emergency measures

Sometimes, despite all your protection protocols and compassionate intent, you will come across a belligerent entity that catches you unawares. 'The Golden Net of Hephaestus' is a technique for dealing with such aggressive entities. Visualise throwing an imaginary golden net over it, in the manner of a Roman gladiator, or perhaps Spiderman if you prefer. This stops the entity in its tracks, allowing you then to regroup and project peace and compassion at it before proceeding with release procedures.

Hephaestus is the Greek equivalent of the Roman Vulcan, the god of blacksmithing, metalworking and volcanoes. Hephaestus made the weapons for the gods in Olympus and was married to Aphrodite.[11] On discovering that she was having an affair with Ares, the god of war, he fashioned a golden net of unbreakable chain-link so fine as to be invisible and ensnared them as they lay in bed together. He then dragged them to Mount Olympus to shame them in front of the rest of the gods.

Chapter 8

Environmental Remediation

The health and well-being of human beings is intimately tied to the earth on which they live and to its radiation. Once this is clearly understood, a door will be opened to a healthier, happier existence for everyone and diseases which threaten them like nightmares will disappear.

-- DR ERNST HARTMANN

The most obvious solution to geopathic stress issues is to move the bed or office desk away from any stress lines so that we do not spend any length of time over the geopathic influence, but in many cases this is not possible due to room constraints. In these situations, a good dowser can provide remedial work using a variety of methods. There are three main approaches to dealing with the problem:

1. Diverting, releasing, or blocking the geopathic stress using focused intent, earth acupuncture with wooden or metal wands, stones, crystals, and suchlike; or shielding with specific materials.
2. Blanketing/masking the problem using an overlay of different energy from a device such as a Raditech, Helios Harmoniser, Bailey Stressbuster, Blueshield etc.
3. Transmutation of the detrimental energy frequencies using dowsing, intent, radionics methods, crystals, orgonite pyramids etc.

The earth acupuncture method is perhaps the most common technique and is used by many dowsers today. It involves placing metal rods, wands, standing stones or other devices at dowsed nodal points around the property to rebalance the energetic matrix of the Earth, in the same way that a medical acupuncturist used needles to balance the energy meridians of the human body. The action of inserting the pins into the Earth forms a conduit for the intent of the dowser to re-pattern the local etheric matrix, releasing any points or lines of stress and preventing it from entering the property.

The second method involves placement of high-tech (and often expensive) proprietary devices that purport to dampen or mask the geopathic stress inside the home or office by overlaying different energy frequencies, for example Schumann Resonators that broadcast the natural 7.83Hz resonant frequency of the Earth. In certain circumstances, such as an urban apartment building where either there is no access to land, or where you need to be considerate of other building inhabitants, these devices may be the only recourse. However, I feel that these devices are essentially treating the symptoms, not curing the underlying problem. It's like taking painkillers all the time for a persistent migraine, instead of identifying the cause of the headaches. If the primary stressor is not removed from the system, then that system remains compromised and under stress, and any healing modality will be rendered less effective as long as that stressor remains.

The third method relies on neutralising the detrimental energy frequencies to a harmless state or even transmuting them into beneficial energies using dowsing methods of focused intent and visualisation, or by applying more technological fixes such as radionic broadcast devices, orgonite pyramids or crystals. Often this can be done remotely without the practitioner even visiting the property, even if the property is in another part of the world. All that the dowser requires is a good plan of the property to work on, and things are made even easier today with online aids such as Google Earth and maps. Many practitioners actually prefer to work remotely, regarding it as safer practice. Personally, I choose to adopt a more 'hands-on' approach and work on-site if possible, as I find that there is almost always something in the local environment that might be missed if I am working remotely, or some piece of information that I will only get from talking with the client face to face.

There is something of a fuzzy boundary between all three approaches, depending on circumstances and the particular expertise of the dowser. Every situation is different, and often a combination of techniques is required to achieve resolution. Most issues can be cleared in a single visit or, at most, a short succession of visits spaced over a period of weeks. If the client is seeing a holistic practitioner, then a further check with them afterwards is recommended to ensure that the work has been successful.

Of the three approaches, I personally find that the first method is the best long-term solution as it attempts to remove the energy from the space (or at least prevent it from entering). With the other two methods, the energy is still present, although either suppressed (2) or transmuted (3). My primary 'go-to' method of treatment remains earth acupuncture in some form or other, wherever possible. Typically, for energy lines I will perform temporary acupuncture using wooden wands, often in conjunction with flower essences or some other elemental aid to assist and speed up the process. Copper pipe is also useful on energy lines if I need to leave something in place permanently.

Energy lines can be diverted if necessary, either around or over the house, using one or more standing stones or even stone garden features such as a birdbath or sundial plinth, correctly placed. When sited over a detrimental vortex, such as the crossing of two underground water veins, these structures are also useful in grounding the energy – indeed this configuration of crossed water veins is frequently found under single standing stones. The presence of some organic material, such as animal bones, either within or buried underneath these stones, as a ceremonial act, will enhance their function in this regard.[1]

For geopathic water lines, there is no denying that permanent acupuncture with steel rods hammered into the ground is the most effective remedy. I carry two or three lengths of 12mm (1/2 inch) rod and will dowse the appropriate length to use once on site. Steel reinforcing rod for concrete (rebar) is a suitable material for this, and you can find this at building supply stores or online. Many suppliers will also cut the bar to your specified length. Smaller lengths of welding rod can also be useful, and I use these as temporary acupuncture needles for fine-tuning work and remediating passive human-held place memory issues.

Healing methods vary depending on each situation, and a good dowser should have a variety of methods available in their toolkit. Crystals are useful for directing and transmuting subtle energy and, in a city environment where there is no access to land to work on, crystals on the window ledge or floor of the apartment where the stress lines enter can provide a reasonable solution. The drawbacks are that they require more maintenance than other methods (most crystals need regular cleansing) and, if used indoors they are easily moved or lost, particularly if the client has pets or small children. But there are ways around this. In my regular toolkit, I have some pre-made sealed copper pipes containing inexpensive crystal chips, bought from a garden centre. The pipes can also be filled with crystals, rock dust, or other substances to suit. Copper stop ends are useful for sealing the pipes, and I also have a few pipe clips in case I need to fix one someplace indoors, for example under a window ledge or along a skirting board. These pre-made 'matrix wands' make effective placeholders to anchor your focused intention. I also carry a few random lengths of copper pipe and fixings plus a small hacksaw so that I can cut them to the correct (dowsed) length to make a matrix wand on site if necessary. Thin copper tubing, used to feed radiators in central heating systems, can be bent into a semicircle or horseshoe shape and placed, points down, across the centre of the stress line inside the building (dowse to see what length is needed and how far apart to make the points). Another fix that I sometimes employ involves pre-made copper wire spirals, perhaps with a crystal held in the centre if it dowses appropriate to use such, placed inside an empty electrical switch box with a blanking plate on the front. Again, these can be fixed to the wall or skirting board at floor level. Of course, these 'widgets' don't get maintained by the client so I don't regard them as a permanent fix, and follow-up visits might be required in future to keep everything working properly.

I frequently use crystals as a temporary fix when staying away from home, particularly in hotel rooms. Some quartz points and a few lumps of black tourmaline can be remarkably effective at moving an energy line aside from the bed or reducing its intensity to manageable levels. An easy technique involves placing the quartz point in the centre of the energy line with the pointed end facing 'downstream'. Then, holding the intention that you are 'turning down' the energy, slowly rotate the crystal 90 degrees until it lies perpendicular to the line -

imagine that you are turning down the volume on your hi-fi. This reduces the width of the energy line to a narrow band, which is then easily block with some black tourmaline. I also place tourmaline at the ends of the quartz crystal to soak up any scatter. Tourmaline is a very versatile grounding crystal and is one of the few that doesn't require regular cleansing. In the morning, you simply reverse the process by picking up the tourmaline, then 'turn up' the volume until the quartz crystal is again pointing down the length of the energy line, before lifting it away.

Another effective outdoor treatment is to scatter handfuls of quartz fragments across the stressed line next to the wall of the house. Provided these will be subjected to the occasional rain shower, they won't then require much maintenance, other than to make sure they are not removed. Many excavated stone circles and cairns contain substantial amounts of white quartzite fragments; these seem to exert a harmonising effect on the energy, and larger rocks with a high quartz content can be amazingly effective at blocking geopathic stress lines. Crieff-based dowser David Cowan records how just such a line of large white quartzite stones protects Drummond Castle in Perthshire from geopathic energies arising from a geological fault.[2]

In North America, many dowsers utilise the 'magic blue tape' method, which seems peculiar to that continent as I have not encountered it elsewhere. This simply uses a strip of painters' blue masking tape of suitable dowsed length, applied topically under the carpet inside the house, or buried in the ground outside, placing it lengthwise along the affected water line. I don't use this method myself and would regard it as a temporary fix only, but it's worth experimenting with.

These are just a selection of methods employed to treat geopathic stress, and every dowser has their own favourite way of working. Ultimately, it comes down to the intent of the dowser; the rest is largely just props and ceremony. A dowser should always be able to operate with whatever tools are available at the time and, after you've been doing this sort of clearing work for a while, you become rather good at improvising. In Chapter 6, I reported on a very effective landscape healing performed in British Columbia by myself and a group of local energy workers, where the final clearing was performed by a dowser scattering the contents of a herbal teabag across the offending stress line!

Basics of earth acupuncture

Temporary acupuncture is appropriate in cases of light geopathic stress or unbalanced energy lines. These energies are highly amenable to being blessed using temporary acupuncture methods. Energy lines are extremely subtle in nature and have a gentler energy compared to underground water veins. They fluctuate in size and placement to a certain degree according to the phase of the moon, season of the year, and even vary between day and night, so it is seldom appropriate to try to permanently fix them in place unless you are constructing a sacred space.

For most temporary work on energy lines, leys or grids – I use wooden wands, or (rarely) a copper rod if something more heavy-duty is required, often augmented with some elemental aid such as a flower essence or a tuning fork. Steel should never be used on an energy line as it causes too much disruption. I have a selection of wooden wands and will dowse which one to use at each location, how long to leave it for, and whether the process can be helped along by adding a vibrational essence.

Choosing a wand

You can easily harvest wands yourself from appropriate trees and craft them to your own specifications. Traditionally, a wand should be about as thick as your thumb and the length from the outside of your bent elbow to the tip of your middle finger — this is the ancient measurement of the cubit. Connect with the tree spirit using your dowsing, and ask if it is happy to gift you a wand to aid you in your work. Then dowse which branch is suitable, tell the tree that you would like to use that particular branch, and ask if it will imbue some of its own energy into the section that you plan to use. Dowse how long you should wait before cutting the branch to allow time for that to happen, and be sure to thank the tree afterwards, perhaps leaving it with a little offering.

Tree lore is deeply entrenched in European cultures and working in this way with one of the sacred trees is hugely rewarding. In the old Celtic lunar calendar, there are 13 sacred trees, one for each of the months. In the Druid tradition, tree names are also associated with the *ogham* alphabet and were thought to have originally been used as a mnemonic device. This alphabet is usually based around 20 trees, but there are several modern variations that include up to 25 characters. Wands associated with each letter and carved with the appropriate ogham symbol can be used for divination rather like the Nordic runes and would make a powerful set of wands. However, some woods (vine, ivy, broom) may not make durable wands, and in any case it is not necessary to have so many. I only have half a dozen or so, gathered over the years. These include birch, ash, rowan, hazel, holly, and oak, and of these I use maybe three or four most frequently. But if you are interested in starting a collection, here is a listing of the 13 trees of the lunar calendar and their associations:

Tree	Dates	Symbolism
Birch	24 Dec - 20 Jan	Cleansing, purifying, softening
Rowan	21 Jan - 17 Feb	Boundaries, psychic protection
Ash	18 Feb – 17 Mar	Stimulating, yang, solar
Alder	18 Mar – 14 Apr	Protection, passion, motivation
Willow	15 Apr – 12 May	Intuition, creativity, psychic power
Hawthorn	13 May – 9 Jun	Defence, protection, insight
Oak	10 Jun – 7 Jul	Fortitude, courage, stability
Holly	8 Jul – 4 Aug	Protection, unifying, balance
Hazel	5 Aug – 1 Sep	Wisdom, transformation, knowledge
Vine	2 Sep – 29 Sep	Prophecy, inspiration, truth
Ivy	30 Sep – 27 Oct	Restriction, binding, introspection
Reed	28 Oct – 23 Nov	Cleansing, harmony, divination
Elder	24 Nov – 23 Dec	Regeneration, wisdom, fairy energy

Temporary earth acupuncture

For each energy line requiring treatment, dowse the best location to insert your wand. Is it upstream or downstream of the house? Do you need one each side? Is one wand in the centre of the line appropriate, or should you needle both edges of the line? Which wand(s) from your collection would be most suitable? Which line do you need to work on first?

Having established the order of events, squat down beside the line and, using the wand as a pointer with your pendulum in the other hand, slowly move the wand across the line as you dowse for the exact centre. Then insert the wand into the ground as you visualise yourself channelling healing energy through the wand into the earth. Gently manipulate the wand during this process to stimulate the flow of *chi*, until your pendulum indicates that you have sent enough, then remove your hand, leaving the wand in place.

At this stage, if you have done it correctly, you can often see the wand emitting a faint flame-like plume of energy from its tip, looking similar to the heat haze that you see over a fire or a hot road surface. This is the *sha chi*, or detrimental energy, discharging from the line.

Next, dowse how long you need to leave the wand in place, then dowse to see if the application of some elemental aids (flower essences, tuning fork, incense sticks, crystals etc.) will speed things up, and apply as indicated. Typically, applying one or more flower essences to the tip of the wand dramatically hastens the process. Dowse through your collection and pull out any that come up as being helpful, then dowse how many drops of each to apply and in what order.[3]

Permanent earth acupuncture

For permanent earth acupuncture, the procedure is essentially the same, except that if you are leaving a metal rod in place you should make sure it is in an area where it is not likely to be disturbed and is sunk well below the surface. As you insert the rod, spend a little time working it in your hand like an acupuncture needle, all the while channelling healing energy into the earth, visualising the healthy energy flowing down the line and filling the property with light. Continue with this visualisation while you hammer the rod into the ground. Use another rod as an extension to hammer it beneath the surface. You will develop a sense of how far to insert the rod; usually 10-15cm (5 or 6 inches) below ground level is enough.

Try to make your insertions somewhere out of the way, like in a flower bed or close to the edge of the property, where they are not likely to be disturbed barring serious excavations. Generally, you should work upstream of the stressed area but, in some instances, you may need to pin the flow both upstream and downstream of the property. We can't always be sure that our fix will not adversely affect areas downstream of our working zone, and it is possible that something downstream is quite happy with the energy flow as it is. If you really can't find a suitable location on the line itself, it's possible to work away from the stressed area and focus your healing intention towards it as you manipulate the rod like an acupuncture needle.

But before you start enthusiastically hammering in steel rods everywhere, you first need to check that the area is free of any buried utilities – pipes, drains, electrical cables and so forth. Mistakes here can be expensive, and even dangerous if you happen to rupture a gas or electric feed (this is one of the reasons why you *must* carry comprehensive liability insurance if you are operating professionally). Should the property owner be unable to provide any information and online research prove fruitless, see if your dowsing can offer any insights.

Once, when excavating the bank of a sloping lawn to install a labyrinth, I encountered a steel pipe or bar running out of the bank at roughly a 45° angle and disappearing into the area where the outer path of the labyrinth would lie. Work stopped as I tried to figure out what this could be. It was going to be a massive job if we had to excavate deeply to reroute or rebury the pipe. I thought it most likely to be water or gas, but the owner assured us that all the house utilities were at the other side of the garden, and that this was probably just a bit of old stuff from the building's industrial past that had been left in the ground. In the absence of any better intelligence, I decided to dowse it. Finally, after much questioning with my pendulum, I concluded that it was an old water pipe that was no longer in use, and that it was disconnected at least at one end. I confidently declared that it was safe to cut and handed the hacksaw to the contractor...! Fortunately, the pipe did turn out to be empty, and we soon had the offending ends bent and buried out of the way.

The only occasion when I will leave a permanent fix protruding above ground level is where I leave a copper pipe with some crystals inside and wish to reapply flower essences or other elemental aids at a later date. I will place this in a discrete location under a hedge or somewhere that it's not likely to be disturbed, and protect it with a removable stop end cap, so that it can be easily topped up in the future.

Space Clearing

In extreme cases, it may be appropriate to reinforce the earth acupuncture work by applying space-clearing techniques within the property. Most space-clearing methods are directed towards healing the psycho-spiritual aspects of the space – the stagnant energies, predecessor chi and so on - and, like earth acupuncture, will involve the use of elemental aids like smudging, drumming, vibrational essences, fire ceremonies and similar. Many techniques can be employed, but space-clearing is a larger discipline in itself for which there are several books already available. If you are interested, I suggest checking out the work of Denise Linn and Karen Kingston.

It can be beneficial in the final stage of a consultation to work with the client on setting their intention for the space by performing a fire ceremony or similar ritual, but not all clients are receptive to this idea, so it's wise to assess the need for this on a case by case basis.

There is little doubt that space-clearing will accelerate the healing process and I used to do this as a matter of course as the final part of a consultation; however it is time-consuming to perform, requires you to carry a larger toolkit, and adds at least an hour onto an already lengthy visit. I now only conduct a space-clearing if it's clear from advance work on the space and discussions with the client that one is necessary. In most cases, providing the dowsing ceremony has been performed correctly, balance returns naturally over the course of a few days.

Chapter 9

Practical House Healing

> *Where plants perish and animals are absent, there you also should not live, the place is unhealthy. You will experience disharmony and lose your poise. When you, however, find the place where happy, vital and healthy people live, and many old folk in good health, then stay there, you will soon do without medicine or physician. The mysterious forces of Earth make you healthy.*

> *-- MICHEL NOSTRADAMUS*

In this chapter I shall try to provide an overview of a typical consultation process from start to finish. This is the way that I work, but other people will have different techniques. I also conduct surveys for technopathic issues using scientific measuring equipment as part of a consultation, and it is obviously impossible to do this remotely. Not all dowsers do this latter work as it requires a considerable amount of technical knowledge about electromagnetic issues as well as a selection of measuring apparatus. I have a background as a production electrician in the entertainment industry, so I do know what I am talking about (most of the time!). I find this type of survey to be essential these days to eliminate any technopathic problems, as the symptoms of technostress can be almost identical to those of geopathic stress, and it's important to address both.

Of course, it's not always possible to visit a property if it's located at a considerable distance or even in another country, and in such cases, we must rely on dowsing methods alone. Some people prefer to work entirely remotely and achieve excellent results without leaving their own workspace. The advantages to this approach are that a) you can work from the safety of your own psychically protected space, and b) it saves a lot of time and travel expense! However, I place immense value on meeting and talking to the client in person. It creates a better rapport and you often pick up on something that was not apparent from email communications or phone conversations. Being present on site also enables a stronger connection with the spirit of place.

The Initial Approach

Whatever method a prospective client uses to reach out to you, the first thing to do is to ask them to describe, in their own words, exactly what the problem is. This often takes place during a phone conversation or via email but, to achieve consistency and a proper case study, I ask them to complete a short questionnaire well in advance of my visit. In addition to asking the names and ages of everyone in the house, it includes questions about the type and age of the property, history of previous use and inhabitants (if known), number of rooms, any recent building work, either on the house or in the local area, and size of garden (or land). Clients are also asked to provide a plan of the house showing function of each room (with separate plans for each floor of the house), and a garden plan. Plans are more effective if they are hand-drawn by the client as this provides an energetic 'witness' that helps connect you to the site. They don't need to be completely accurate or even to scale, provided they show the room layout and indicate the direction of North. For reference, each room should be labelled showing its function, but it's not necessary to detail every fixture or item of furniture. For practical purposes, I find normal A4 size paper easiest to work with. Architect's plans can work provided they are of a reasonable size and not too heavily annotated but, since they often contain a great deal of extraneous information, I actually prefer to have a plan that is hand-drawn by the client. If you do have to work with an architect's plan, get the client to sign or otherwise write something in the margin to provide your witness to them and the property.

I also ask if there is anything unusual about the behaviour of animals in and around the property; if there are any areas of poor plant growth (including houseplants), whether any areas of the house feel consistently cold or 'heavy', which may indicate psychic disturbances, and ask them do describe, in their own words, what specific concerns they have and why they have asked for a consultation.

Armed with this information, and before doing any dowsing, I spend some time researching the property online. There are several websites that can provide useful information on the history of the property, geology of the area, locations of any quarries, mines, power lines, rivers, rail lines, major roads and so forth in the vicinity - all of which may contribute to geopathic stress in the property. In the UK, there are online interactive maps from the Coal Authority that will show any historical mining activity in the area, and the British Geological Survey has interactive maps with overlays displaying area geology, boreholes, earthquake activity, and other useful information. You can also check old maps to see when the property was built and what existed on site beforehand (this can often affect the energies of the present structure), whether there are any wells, and so on. Sometimes, you can even find old county records online that provide useful information about previous site history. For technopathic issues, there are some websites that will show you the location of any nearby phone masts although, with the speed at which 5G is proliferating, these are increasingly out of date, and those few that are regularly updated inevitably require a subscription to access.

Google and other map sites displaying satellite imagery and aerial photography of the area are useful both in providing an overview of the landscape, and for map dowsing. Google Street View can even provide a visual and energetic connection to the property, providing that it is visible of course. In the UK we are also blessed with the wonderful Ordnance Survey maps, which will show many features such as historic churches and ancient sites you might otherwise overlook. It's well worth paying their very reasonable annual subscription so that you can access these online, and on your smartphone or tablet when you are out and about. The US equivalent is the USGS topographical maps, which are available online, but they do not include as much detail as the OS maps.

You should make use of these online facilities as much as possible, and search for other information where you can find it. The local library can often provide historical and other details of a property. This all helps paint a picture of the property and the area and will often throw up something unusual that you may need to consider when you physically dowse the property.

I had a client in St Louis who asked me to work on his office. As I'm based in Scotland, this would clearly need to be a remote consultation. During my research, I discovered that East St Louis is the site of the largest concentration of pre-Columbian native American mounds in north America, a major city known as Cahokia.[1] I had no knowledge of this before I started researching the area, and it transpired that not only was the property in question aligned with several of the mounds, there was some psychic disturbance and a spirit presence directly related to one mound in particular that had to be appeased and relocated. This would never have arisen had I not spent time looking at online map resources.

Checklists

Now it's time to get into our dowsing zone and sit down with the plans to see what we can find. Every dowser has their own preferred checklists; these will be modified and expanded over time, and it can be daunting when starting out to decide what needs to be included and what can be safely ignored. Experience is your best teacher here. There will be occasions when you come across something that you're not familiar with, and you have to step back and go through some dowsing questions to ascertain what it is you are dealing with. For this reason, it's better to learn by apprenticing with a more experienced dowser or attend a proper training course – there is only so much that you can learn from a book. Over time, your checklist will grow to accommodate the new knowledge you've gained through dowsing. The best advice I can give in this regard is to work on the old 'KISS' principle – *Keep It Simple, Stupid!* Start with the basic earth energies picture of yin and yang chi flows – water and energy leys – and go from there. How many water lines are affecting the property? Do they originate from blind springs (domes) or downshafts? If so, can you access these points in the garden? What's their direction of flow? How much geopathic stress do they carry? (Here you can use a percentage scale, a 1-10 rating, some other chart like von Pohl's 1-16 ranking, or Bovis units if you work with those). How many energy leys affect the space? Are they stressed, and if so, how much? What about serpentine energy lines? Earth grids? Do you need to check for vortices and portals? What else could you be checking for?

Before sitting down to dowse through your checklist, make sure that you are grounded and protected as described in Chapter 5, and that you have gone through the advanced protocol and are ready to dowse. After asking your three "Can I? May I? Should I?" questions, sit with the property plan on the table in front of you, place your free hand on the plan, and dowse, "Do I have a connection to this place?" You should of course get a 'yes' to this, but if not, then devise some further questions to uncover the blockage. Perhaps this case is not for you? Maybe there is some vital piece of information missing, or it's just not the right time for you to dowse this and you need to try again later? Bear in mind that, at this stage, we are simply trying to determine what's happening, and it's a purely diagnostic exercise. Later we will work proactively to bring balance to the space, either by dowsing remotely, or when we visit the property to work on-site. Of course, we cannot foresee every possible situation so there are always more questions to be asked; however, a basic checklist is shown below as an example:

Dowsing Checklist		
Item	*Result*	*Notes*
Water lines		
Blind springs/downshafts?		
Energy leys		
Serpent lines		
Other lines		
Grids – Curry, Hartmann, Benker, other?		
Vortices/Portals?		
Human discarnates		
Elemental activity		
Nature spirits		
Trolls		
Site guardians		
Devas		
Aliens		
Demons/entities		
Thought forms (curses)		
Magic or ritual use		
Drug or alcohol use		
Boundary issues		
Power objects		
Murder, suicide, other human trauma		
Other (specify)		

The checklist provides a basic outline of topics that you could dowse for, but don't allow yourself to be limited by this, and feel free to add or delete items as you will, according to your own frame of reference. You may need to ask other questions for each topic, depending on the initial results.

Physical environment checklist

Physical environment and previous site use			
Phone masts		Road works	
Power lines		Building sites	
Substations		Hospitals	
Major roads		Cemeteries	
Railways		Crematoria	
Tunnels		Megalithic sites	
Quarries etc.		Castles or forts	
Mines or caves		Church / sacred space	
Wells		Other (specify)	

Geology:

It's also useful at this stage to make notes about the physical environment of the property, and this table should be pretty self-explanatory. Clearly, you want to know about any major land disturbances that might affect the earth energies of the area, and you also want to know about any nearby phone masts or power lines that may be exerting technopathic influences. Previous site use can be checked by viewing old maps of the area, but other things may have to be dowsed, for example tunnels, mines or caves which may not be identified on maps. You can also dowse in advance for things like road works, construction works, phone masts and such like, although you can (and should) also visually check these on site as part of your visit. Once again, leave room for that undefined 'other'. You can never be sure whether something has been overlooked.

Map Dowsing

Having completed the checklist, the next step is to move on to dowsing the floorplan of the property and plotting the affected areas. Map dowsing techniques were covered in detail in *Dowsing Magic – Book One*, but I will briefly summarise them here. You will need a pen or pencil to use as a pointer in your free hand in addition to your dowsing tool. For me, a pendulum works best for map dowsing, but you can of course use a different tool if you are more comfortable with something else. I find that my pendulum functions equally well in my non-dominant hand, which allows me to write notes as I work through the procedure.

Water and serpentine energy lines

Find a convenient edge of the property or plan at which to begin. Dowse whether the line crosses this edge. If the answer is affirmative, move your pointer slowly along the edge whilst keeping your dowsing tool moving in the search position, asking the tool to react when the pointer crosses the line. Mark this with a 'X'. Now, start moving the pointer in a series of arcs extending outwards from that point, again asking your dowsing tool to react where it crosses the line. Continue marking each point in turn until you can connect them with a meandering line across the property showing the route of the water or energy flow (Fig. 18).

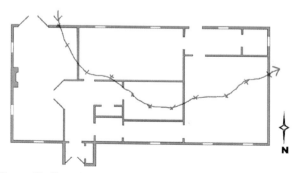

Figure 18: Floorplan showing water line

Dowse to find the direction of flow and percentage of geopathic stress (if any) on the line. Repeat for other lines and make a note of these results.

Energy leys and grids

Proceed as for water, marking the point at which the line crosses the edge of the plan. Dowse to see what other edge it crosses, then dowse along that edge until you get a reaction. Mark that point, then draw a straight line connecting it to the first

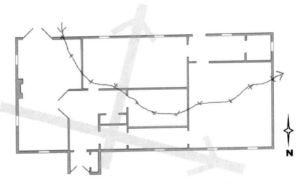

Figure 19: Floorplan with two added energy leys

point. You may also like to dowse the width of the lines, marking in the edges (Fig. 19).

If your checklist has indicated any problematic grids, do some dowsing to ascertain what these are. Usually it will be a crossing point of two double-strength negative lines. You don't need to draw in the whole grid, just show the problematic lines. In the illustration (Fig. 20), I've shown a crossing point of two lines of the Curry grid

Again, dowse for direction of flow and magnitude of geopathic stress for each line that you find.

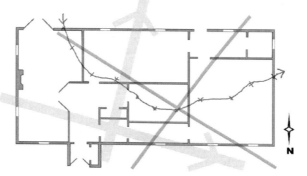

Figure 20: Added negative Curry grid crossing

Vortices, portals, other point sources

For things that are a single point source, such as vortices, interdimensional portals, power objects, discarnates and so on, it's easy enough to ascertain the affected areas by dowsing each room in turn asking, "is there a ... here?" (Fig. 21).

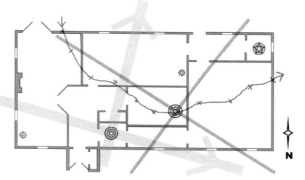

Figure 21: Added vortex points, a portal, and power objects

In this example, you can see there is a detrimental vortex located at the Curry grid crossing, which coincides with the water vein. This would be a very unhealthy place to put a bed.

There is another vortex where the energy leys cross, two power objects in separate rooms, and an interdimensional portal of some sort in the south-west corner. This looks like it could be a big job!

Having worked through your checklist and map-dowsed the plan of the property, mentally visualise placing a protective circle around it to seal it from any other influences until you can carry out the work. This is particularly important in cases exhibiting spiritual disturbances, as many discarnates and other entities may leave or otherwise conceal themselves from you when you visit, only to return once you have left. Of course, if you are working purely from a remote perspective, this protective circle would be the concluding part of the operation, and you would probably wish to physically draw a circle around the plan to reinforce your intent.

The next step is to establish the healing modality required to balance the space.

Remedial Procedures

Ultimately, the actual healing of the space comes down to the application of focused intention and blessing through the dowsing system that we have established. How this is practically implemented will obviously vary depending on each situation and whether you are working remotely or on-site, but the general procedure is a five-step process that runs something like this:

1. Invitation

First, affirm your invitation to work on the site. Check to ensure that you have all the necessary permissions from the client(s), your spirit guides and your higher self. Use your dowsing at this stage to attain clarity about the work. Is it the right task for you at this time? Can you manage it on your own? How long is it likely to take? This invitation process begins as soon as you decide to work on the project and proceeds up to the point when you commence the work. During this time, pay attention to any day-signs, synchronicities, imagery, feelings, dreams, visions, and other divinatory signals that come to you about the job, particularly those that occur on the day of your visit. Spirit moves into matter through pattern and form, so you will often gain inspiration from unexpected sources. The more you do this sort of work, the more such day-signs will manifest to you. It could be a flight of birds overhead, a dream, a television program relating to your project, a piece of music, or a significant landscape feature that you notice as you are travelling to the job. Anything can be a day-sign.

2. Preparation

Even before reaching the site, you can be checking in with the local matrix to get a feel for the area and the work to be done. You should have mentally prepared yourself before setting off by performing a grounding meditation and working through the dowsing and protection protocol described in Chapter 5. I usually begin my dowsing questions even as I am driving to the client, using deviceless dowsing methods (my favourite whilst driving is to rub a thumb on the side of my forefinger, a 'yes' response is when it sticks, a 'no' response is when it doesn't stick).

If you are working on-site, spend some time discussing with the client specific concerns and symptoms that they and other inhabitants are experiencing. Are the symptoms constant or intermittent, recurring at particular times? Do they only happen in a particular place? How long have they been going on? Is everyone affected? Questions like this help you confirm (or refute) your advance dowsing findings and identify the causes of any problems, as well as allowing you time to settle into the space. This is where you need to develop a good bedside manner and usually involves a cup of tea with the client. During this conversation, I keep my pendulum running in constant 'search mode', as a change in its motion can indicate some area of trauma that needs addressing.

Ask the client to show you around the house to familiarise yourself with the layout and get a feel for the space. Don't do any dowsing at this point but do open your awareness for any energetic changes. Sudden drops in room temperature or feelings of other presences might suggest a spirit manifestation of some sort; a resistance to passing through a doorway might be indicative of boundary stress; a sense of being stared at could be emanating from a power object, and so on. At this stage, I am usually checking for technopathic stress issues with an armload of meters and making notes on a clipboard so it can be difficult to maintain psychic sensitivity, but with practice it becomes easier.

It's vitally important after this that you now have peace and quiet to begin your dowsing. Many clients are curious about the process and will ask if they can watch, but this is likely to impact detrimentally on your dowsing so resist the temptation. There will be time to demonstrate dowsing for them later on.

Find a safe place to begin your dowsing session, preferably outside in the garden somewhere. Ask your spirit guides or use your dowsing tool to locate a neutral area in which to begin. Repeat your grounding and centring visualisation, making sure that your personal energy field is clear and filled with light. At this stage you should also connect with your spirit team and invoke any other helpful spirits that you feel you can work with, such as Pan or Herne, Archangels Michael, Raphael, Gabriel or Uriel, or perhaps a locally-recognised deity, saint, or other spirit being who is willing to help.

After extending your energy field over the area, initiate a dialogue with the Spirit of Place and introduce yourself to any other dominant local spirits such as site guardians, landscape devas, nature spirits or whatever presents itself to you. Imagine a conversation where you ask something like, "I'm (name), I am here in the spirit of love and harmony to bring healing and balance to this space. Am I welcome, and are you willing to work with me?" You need to establish what your relationship is with these beings, whether they are willing to work with you on healing the space, and what is required from you in return.

Spend some time at this stage checking in with the various levels of consciousness associated with the site, working up to planetary consciousness (Gaia) if needed. You are here in service and need to work in harmony with these beings, not arrogantly impose your will on the proceedings. It's a co-creative process. Frequently something you had not previously thought of will come to mind during this tuning in period, so don't rush things and leave five or ten minutes for other factors to manifest. This is usually where inspiration will strike and show you the way forward.

3. Evaluation

Now it is time to physically dowse the site, updating your remote assessment of it. What items on your checklist require work? Is there anything else that has arisen since you arrived? Is there anything unexpected or surprising? Examine the Lower,

Middle, and Upper realms of existence, looking for any areas of stagnation, pollution, disturbances, patterns of trauma.

Establish the order of work and what needs to be attended to first. If there are any discarnates or other psycho-spiritual disturbances, then you almost always need to deal with these first as they may attach to the client or yourself if you deprive them of their energy source. However, in rare cases the reverse is true, so always check the most appropriate order in which to work. From your checklist, you will have a fair idea of the other areas requiring attention – the water veins, energy leys, grids, vortices, interdimensional portals, power objects, boundary issues and so forth. Also check again to see if there is anything else that you have missed or overlooked.

Once you have completed the site evaluation, it's helpful to engage the client by explaining your findings at this stage. You can map the routes of features such as water veins and energy leys in the garden using marker flags and/or string, and most clients will be pleased to see this (some even want to take pictures). For larger sites, I sometimes also map the lines on my phone using the GPS plotting app Dowsing Mapper, which displays your findings in a Google Earth placemark file that you can afterwards send to the client.[2] It's a little tricky to operate this as you are dowsing, so I prefer to mark everything out before then recording my findings on the app.

If your client is open to the idea, you can also allow them to try dowsing a water or energy line themselves, and even dowse the size of their aura or muscle-test them both off and on the line to demonstrate its effect on their body. This is an excellent way to instil confidence in your work, especially if you repeat the exercise after you have completed your remedial healing of the space.

4. Ceremony

If you are guided to perform any spirit release of discarnates or do other psycho-spiritual realigning as the first part of the healing process, then return to your safe spot and do that using the methods described in Chapter 7. Remember to close any portals afterwards by visualising them closing as you pull the edges together, or erase the portal by wiping over it with one hand, then seal with an appropriate sacred symbol such as a cross or pentagram.

Next, carry out the earth acupuncture work. Dowse what lines to work on first, and whether each one requires temporary or permanent acupuncture. I usually work on the energy lines first using temporary pins and leave those in place while I perform the permanent acupuncture on the stressed water lines. After that, I check on the temporary wands and remove if they have finished working, then conduct another dowsing check around the site to ensure that the work has been effective. Some fine-tuning with smaller pins might be in order to heal any muddy zones of human-held psychic trauma or predecessor chi but, as always, this is dependent on the situation. If warranted, now is the time to psychically re-draw the building boundary, deal with any remaining minor disturbances, and carry out any space-clearing inside - remembering to check for any power objects if these came up on your checklist. Deal with these using visualisation and the steps described in the dowsing protocol from Chapter 5 to neutralise detrimental energy patterns, before flooding the object with white light.

5. Closure

Return to your safe spot and run through your checklist to make sure that you have covered everything necessary. With any psycho-spiritual issues, check that nothing is hiding or confusing you – this is a common occurrence with entities and discarnate spirits. Declare a challenge three times to confirm. Is there anything that you have missed? Is there anything else to do here? Will you need to return? Is there anything attached to you or your client?

You should never leave the situation unresolved. If you need to abandon the healing process for any reason, try to find a natural break in the procedure, set a mental seal on the work, and return to it as soon as you can. If you dowse that the process is not going to complete during the time of your visit and will require additional help, you can ask your guides to create a self-sustaining energetic 'matrix' that will continue the healing process and remain in place until the work is complete. It's nice to reinforce this with a material component that is then left with the client. This might be a crystal, a flower essence spray that you mix appropriately from your toolkit, a sigil, or some other 'widget'. There may be some other permanent mechanism required to ground the healing, and it's always worth dowsing to see if this is the case. Maybe the client needs to be involved with the process and so you advise them to create a small altar or other sacred space? Perhaps they need to continue smudging the space regularly? Is there a feng-shui cure that they could implement? Follow your inspired thought here and allow yourself to be guided to the most appropriate solution.

Make sure that you communicate your results to the client appropriately, remembering the need to adapt your vocabulary to suit that of the client. Not everyone will relate to your dowsing worldview so you may need to modify your terminology to suit. It's useless to talk about elemental disturbances or fairies at the bottom of the garden to a hard-nosed scientific type - you might instead use terms like 'quantum imbalances', 'geopsychic disturbances' or similar. Although some clients may want to hear about everything you have done in great detail, this can have an adverse effect as people have a tendency to focus overly much on the negative parts and not enough on the wonderful transformative healing energy that you have brought to their space. This can actually result in them unconsciously calling that detrimental energy right back in again, as they have become so accustomed to living with it that they feel something is somehow wrong when it is removed. It is better in such cases to speak in general terms rather than specific. It helps to reinforce the healing in their mind by muscle-testing, or dowsing the aura of, the client over a previously stressed line to demonstrate the change to beneficial energy.

Before you depart, give the job your best blessing and thank your spirit team and other helpers for their work before releasing them. Disconnect yourself using stage three of the dowsing protocol to close any other attachments you have to the space and bring your consciousness back into everyday reality. Finally, have something to eat and/or drink to ensure that you are fully grounded and back in the 'here and now' before leaving. It is easy simply to pack everything into your car and drive away without doing this, but having done it a couple of times myself, I can assure you that you are not safe to be driving in such a mental state! I now always have a pack of oatcakes and some water with me on dowsing jobs for such eventualities.

6. Aftercare

Following the consultation, you should prepare a report on your work and send it to the client, bearing in mind the caveat to adapt your explanatory model to suit the situation and the client. There is always a lot of information for a client to take on board, particularly your recommendations regarding any remedial steps requiring some involvement on their part. It is also useful to include a plan showing the locations of your findings, noting positions of any earth acupuncture points in case they are planning on any future garden remodelling.

It's common for there to be some disturbances in the energetic balance of the property for a few days following a house healing. It is rather analogous to the healing crisis that is frequently experienced during homeopathic treatments, where symptoms appear to worsen before improvements manifest. The property's inhabitants may notice some emotional and psychological changes, such as poor sleep patterns, lethargy and fatigue, muddled thought processes and interpersonal communication problems. There may even be an apparent increase in psychic activity. Often, these are the very symptoms that caused them to engage your services in the first place! Reassure your clients before leaving that such things might occur during the first three or four days following your healing, and advise them to keep hydrated and well-nourished during this period. If the 'settling down period' takes longer than ten days, then it's likely that you have missed something and may need to revisit the site for some further work.

If all goes well, you will hear nothing but praise from your client for your healing work. More subtle changes will manifest over a period of two to three months, and clients often find themselves adjusting their living patterns during this time as new opportunities for using the space emerge. The behaviour of pets may change noticeably, and plant growth is often enhanced. I advise clients not to make any major life decisions wherever possible during this period, especially those relating to the property itself, until the changes have fully taken hold. During this time, you should be available to answer their questions and carry out further work on the space as required. Set a reminder for yourself to check in with them again after this period to see if they have any remaining concerns.

Working Remotely

The techniques of distant assessment and healing are to all intents and purposes identical to those for on-site work; the only difference lies in how you creatively adapt your real-life procedures to remote working. As long as you can mentally connect to the target space, you can work effectively.

Treat your plan of the space as a scaled-down witness of the actual site. Mount the plan on some thick card or fibreboard then, where you need to perform some earth acupuncture, you can use steel pins instead of your metal rods, toothpicks instead of wooden wands, copper wire instead of pipe, and so on. Bring as many on-site techniques to the work as you can imagine. You can still apply elemental aids like flower essences, tuning forks, incense sticks, crystals etc. to the working. Mark lines with thread tied between pins, and 'divert' them by re-routing the thread as you apply your intent to the action. Or, you may prefer to simply direct healing intent to the property through the plan, coordinating this with your pendulum spinning in the minimise/decrease motion described in Chapter 5, as you visualise a sieve of white light descending through the property, pulling all the detrimental energy and negativity with it.

To close and 'seal' the operation, try drawing a protective circle around the property using specially prepared ink or water that you have charged with intention and perhaps enhanced with the addition of some flower essence or other vibrational aid. If dowsing suggests that you need to maintain some ongoing work on the space, you can set up an energetic matrix as previously described and reinforce this by enclosing the folded plan in some physical construct. Wrap it in tinfoil or coloured paper, seal it in an envelope along with some crystals or other appropriate aids, sandwich it in a copper spiral wrapped around a sigil, and so on. Be creative, use your imagination and follow your inspired thought to discover the best approach. This can be a lot of fun to do and I am often surprised by the creative avenues that manifest during the procedure. As long as you remain 'in the zone' and follow your dowsing intuition, you will know when the process is complete.

Afterword

> *In a way, we are magicians. We are alchemists, sorcerers, and wizards. We are a very strange bunch. But there is great fun in being a wizard.*
>
> -- *BILLY JOEL*

We have almost reached the end of our exploration into the outer reaches of the dowsing world. When I started this book, I anticipated that it would be much shorter; but condensing decades of experience into one volume has not been easy, especially when considering the need to generalise concepts and terminology to make things as accessible as possible.. I hope that you have enjoyed the journey and, along the way, learned something about the various methods employed by dowsers in the house healing process. If this book encourages you to take the information you need and incorporate it into your own practice (if you are a dowser), or emboldens you to seek out opportunities for further learning (if you are not), then I have succeeded in my task.

At the beginning, I said that this book would not teach you how to heal your home, but it would teach you how I might go about healing your home. As my early spiritual development was grounded in the Western mystery tradition, my dowsing practice perhaps has more of an eclectic and shamanic flavour than most. This doesn't mean that you have to follow this same pattern, and if you come from a more religious background you are likely to draw upon those traditions to provide your working paradigm. A dowser has to feel comfortable within his or her own psychic working space. Use whatever frame of reference you feel most comfortable with, seek out new opportunities to study with different teachers, and practise, practise, practise! You will undoubtedly end up doing things quite differently from me, and that's absolutely fine. Use the techniques that work for you, discard the rest, and develop your own *modus operandi.* There is always more to learn, and as the old saying goes; the more we learn, the more we realise how much there is still to learn. Your dowsing skill is the perfect guide on that journey of exploration.

Indago Felix! (To the fruitful search — the motto of the American Society of Dowsers)

Grahame Gardner
May 2020

Appendix

This is a transcript of an interview by Nobuo Kato for the Japanese health magazine 'Anemone', conducted following the British Society of Dowsers 2013 conference in Cirencester (I was BSD President at the time).

N. The conference was really impressive for me. I was amazed that so many people attended. Do you remember how many?

G. I think we had around 160 this time. The size of our conference has traditionally been limited by the size of the lecture theatre in our favourite venue of the Royal Agricultural University at Cirencester, which has been our home for many years. In 2014 we are moving to Keele University, which has a larger lecture theatre and much better facilities than Cirencester, so we hope it will attract a larger audience.

N. I noticed BSD has four special interest groups - Earth Energies, Water & Services, Health & Wellness, and Archaeology. When did you make such categories and why?

G. The Special Interest Groups (SIGs) evolved from a recognition that some members were primarily interested in a particular area of dowsing and the Society wanted to encourage that. The first one, the Earth Energies Group, was formed in 1995. At this time, the Society was mainly focused on tangible dowsing and did not want to acknowledge the more esoteric areas as it feared it would discredit any scientific understanding of dowsing (this attitude still persists today in some older members). Water was the second SIG to be formed, in 2002, followed by Health & Wellness in 2003 and lastly Archaeology in 2004.

It has proved a mixed blessing at times, as there is a tendency to be too rigid in trying to categorise dowsing into one of the four areas; and it's also an administrative nightmare as each group is run by volunteers and manage their own bank accounts, which are ring-fenced from the main BSD account. We are currently trying to bring more centralisation to the financial arrangements to make them easier to administrate.

N. Which area is most popular and how do you think it will become in future?

G. Earth Energies is by far the most popular at present, followed by Health, then Archaeology, and lastly Water, which has the smallest number of members. That's an interesting dynamic, as most people associate dowsing with locating water sources, yet the vast majority of the membership – over 90% - are interested in the more esoteric areas of dowsing and it is likely to remain that way. If anything, people are becoming interested in ever more esoteric uses like spirituality and psychic development, and dowsing is a fantastically useful tool in those areas.

N. Here's a simple and fundamental question - what is dowsing and what the purpose of it?

G. Historically, dowsing is best known as a technique for finding water sources and minerals, but it is so much more than that. It can be used to locate missing items, find underground archaeological features, pipes, cables and other utilities, track energy currents in the earth, detect illness and analyse disease in the body and much more. Distance is no object to the dowser as it is possible to dowse remotely from a map or plan, or even a photograph. The applications of dowsing are only limited by our ability to conceive of them. I would suggest that it is actually a system for programming your brain. It allows you to gain easier access to your intuitive side, so it can really help you with making decisions in life.

N. In Japan now, people are becoming more interested in geopathic stress – is this true in the UK?

G. Dowsing for geopathic stress has been popular for many years, and not just in the BSD. People started to become aware of it from German research in the 1920s, and even the very early journals of the BSD from the 1930s contain articles about 'noxious earth radiations'. Of course, it is something to consider as part of making sure that our homes are safe places to live in; but there is a tendency for people to focus on these detrimental energies and ignore anything else. There are earth energies that are beneficial to us, for example it can sometimes be good to have an energy ley – these are wide straight flows of subtle *yang*-type energy (water is *yin*) - in our work space, and perhaps we should be more aware of those and less focused on the detrimental. Today, there are more damaging energies we should be worrying about, particularly the increasing use of pulsed microwave radiations from our phones and Wi-Fi systems, and EMF exposure from mains wiring and power lines. The worldwide push to have so-called 'smart meters' installed in every household is only going to increase our exposure to these damaging radiations. All these things need to be considered as part of our overall picture of a healthy home.

N. How do you detect geopathic stress and how do you deal with detrimental energy?

G. By far the easiest way to detect geopathic stress is with dowsing. There are some scientific instruments that can detect small changes in background radiation over geological faults, resistive levels of water in the soil, variations in the geomagnetic field over mineral deposits and so on − all of which can be related to geopathic stress; but such instruments are extremely specialist and very expensive compared to the dowsing rod.

Every dowser has their own favourite technique for dealing with geopathic stress, but generally they will try to either block, divert, or transform the energy so that it is not affecting the property. Sometimes this is done using intent alone, more often a physical aid is employed, such as the earth acupuncture' technique of hammering a metal rod into the earth at a critical node point. Standing stones and more complex structures like 'Power Towers' or 'Cloudbusters' may also be used.

N. Dowsers say that sacred sites are constructed over underground water flows - why is this?

G. Dowsers have demonstrated over many years that sacred spaces like stone circles, temples or (in Europe) pre-Reformation churches and cathedrals are all sited over confluences of water veins known as a blind spring (or a 'dome' in the US), where water is rising towards the surface but not emerging. It is believed that this is particularly energetic water rising from very deep within the earth, not part of the normal hydrological cycle, and is known as 'primary' or 'juvenile' water. Very recently, scientists have discovered that such a deep water source actually exists trapped under great pressure in the Earth's mantle in a mineral called ringwoodite, so it seems that the dowsers were correct all along! In these sacred spaces, the blind spring will frequently have three or more energy leys connected with it, and the leys may even originate or terminate at the blind spring. This combination of leys and blind spring creates what we call a *power centre*. This is why sacred sites such as stone circles, temples, cathedrals and so forth are constructed where they are.

N. Are there good water veins and bad water veins? What is the difference?

G. As Dr Masuro Emoto and some other researchers have demonstrated, water has a memory and can react to human emotions and hold thought patterns. Water veins that carry geopathic stress are usually found to have been energetically polluted by some human activity, such as mining or quarrying, other excavations, siting of electricity substations or poles over the vein, and so on. Water can also carry emotional memory, such as from battle sites or burial grounds. All of these things can produce detrimental energy at the surface, even though the vein may be several feet underground. The energy seems to be generated by interaction between the water and the surrounding rocks, and it rises near-vertically up to and beyond the surface. Surface water in rivers or streams does not produce the same problems.

N. How do you treat electromagnetic pollution? Can we transmute such energy?

G. Electromagnetic pollution is entirely man-made, and the best way to deal with it is to either avoid these emanations if possible or block them using screening materials. High-voltage power lines generate a powerful electromagnetic field, and there are many documented cases of people living close to power lines developing cancers such as leukaemia. Even domestic levels of voltage and current can be harmful if you are close to them, for example if your bed is situated through the wall from the mains electricity box. But levels of EMFs drop off very rapidly with distance in accordance with the inverse square law, so as a rough guide if you are more than one metre away from any electrical sources the exposure is minimal. The higher the voltage, the farther away you need to be, so with the really high voltage power transmission lines a safe distance would be more like 500m.

Other issues in a domestic situation are 'dirty electricity', which is the electronic noise produced by devices like fluorescent lighting, fridges, dimmer switches, switched-mode power supplies and so on that is emitted from the mains wiring as a radio-frequency field; and the increasing use of pulsed microwave radiation in our cordless telephones, Wi-Fi and other digital communications. Such devices will transmit a pulsed signal at full power continuously, and this can be very damaging to the human immune system. You get more exposure from your home Wi-Fi or cordless DECT phone than from a phone mast on the street corner. Many countries, particularly in Europe, are becoming aware of these problems and are limiting the use of Wi-Fi in schools and setting lower power levels for phone masts, but other countries (like the UK) still base their safe levels on thermal effects - in other words the level at which heating of the skin occurs. Yet there is a huge amount of evidence that demonstrates detrimental effects at much lower levels, and although the average exposure may be below the recommended levels, the pulses can be many times higher than the average, and they pulse several times a second. There are two main effects to this – at a biological level, the pulsing affects the ability of our cells to eliminate toxins during sleep, which is when our immune system should be repairing the damage accumulated during the day. At a psychological level, the pulse frequency is in many cases close to some of our natural brain wave frequencies, and this makes it difficult for our brain to switch off' at night. Over time we become more fatigued, our immune systems stop working properly, and chronic ailments develop into more serious disease. The best way to eliminate these problems is to avoid using Wi-Fi and cordless telephones where possible, and to employ some screening materials like carbon paint or metal-impregnated fabric to block any radiations from entering the bedroom. Keeping your bed area clear of electrical appliances is also recommended. Mains filters can also be bought to remove dirty electricity from the house wiring. It may also be possible using intent to transform the energies directly so that they are less detrimental to the human organism, and some dowsers specialise in this. However, personally I think that the energies are too powerful for this and I would rather put my trust in proper shielding methods. There are also many commercial devices on the market that claim to transmute the energies to beneficial and, in certain situations, these may have some benefit.

N. There are many high-rise buildings today… is there a limit to the height that energy grids (Hartmann, Curry etc.) and water veins can influence?

G. Experiments have been conducted in high-rise buildings that demonstrate that the radiations from underground water veins rise near-vertically throughout the entire building. There is a very slight drift eastwards with increased height. Many dowsers say that it is possible to dowse water veins from an airplane, so it seems there is no limit.

N. Could you explain what geomancy is?
G. Geomancy is the art of placing human-built structures on the Earth so that they benefit from the most harmonious

combinations of earth energies. It enhances our connection with Spirit and Place. The Chinese system of feng-shui is a form of geomancy, and indeed most people in the UK struggle to understand geomancy until I say, "It's like Western feng-shui"; indeed many European geomancers will also employ some of the techniques of feng-shui in their work.

Western geomancy is based on three main disciplines: dowsing, sacred geometry, and astronomy/astrology. *Dowsing* lets us detect and analyse the flow of subtle energies within and underneath a building. Almost all of our sacred structures, from the megalithic to the Gothic, are sited over confluences of underground water flows and lines of subtle energy – rising vortices of earth energy that we call power centres. These natural telluric hotspots can be harnessed by the geomancer and used to energise the space. The geomantic act of foundation – 'pinning the dragon' – captures the meandering dragon lines of telluric energy and channels them into the straight flows of yang energy that most people nowadays call ley lines. These emanate out across the landscape, connecting spiritual sites into an invisible network of subtle energy that can be detected through dowsing. *Sacred Geometry* is employed in the construction of the temple space or cathedral to tune the space, enabling the maximum potential of the earth energies. Specific numbers and geometric ratios are employed to impart a subtle, yet palpable, resonance to the structure. It is also important that a space is fully anchored in time and space, and this is where the astronomy/astrology comes in. By designing significant astronomical alignments into the space, we energetically connect it with the celestial energies and create ties with the surrounding landscape. Many churches are aligned to the sunrise on the feast day of their patron saint, and of course many of our megalithic monuments have significant alignments, such as the midwinter solstice at the passage cairn of Newgrange in Ireland, where the rays of the rising sun shine right down the passage to illuminate the end chamber. Japan has many examples of geomancy at work in the placement of shrines and temples, the layout of older towns and ornamental gardens, the veneration of trees and stones and so on. I find geomantic principles to be very prominent in Shinto and traditional Japanese culture.

N. How can we make use of geomancy in our daily life?

G. We can use geomancy in the planning not only of our houses, but in town and country planning – this is an art that is largely lost in Western nations these days, but you can see evidence of geomantic planning in many of our older towns and cities – for example Washington DC in America, or many of Japan's temple districts. On this scale we are channelling the flow of earth energies to benefit the whole area. On a more personal scale, we can use geomantic principles to arrange the harmonious layout of our own homes and gardens, and even our offices. By careful placement of furniture and objects, we can create a personal space that enhances our working and living patterns.

Selected Bibliography

Sue Allen, *Spirit Release – A Practical Handbook*, O Books 2007.

Käthe Bachler, *Earth Radiation - the Startling Discoveries of a Dowser*, Wordmasters 1989.

Christopher Bird, *The Divining Hand*, Whitford Press 1993.

Susan Collins, *Bridge Matter and Spirit with Dowsing*, 2006

David R. Cowan with Anne C. Silk, *Ley Lines of the UK and USA*, Adventures Unlimited Press 2013

Hilda Ellis Davidson, *Lost Beliefs of Northern Europe*, Routledge 1993.

Ivo Dominguez Jr., *Casting Sacred Space - The Core of all Magickal Work*, Weiser 2012.

Janet Farrar & Gavin Bone, *Progressive Witchcraft*, Career Press 2004.

Philip Goff, *Galileo's Error: Foundations for a New Science of Consciousness*, Penguin 2019.

Glennie Kindred, *The Tree Ogham* 1999.

Eliphas Levi, *Transcendental Magic*, trans. A. E. Waite, Weiser 1968.

Dr Patrick MacManaway, *Dowsing for Health*, Lorenz 2001.

Blanche Merz, *Points of Cosmic Energy,* C W Daniel Co 1995.

Alanna Moore, *Touchstones for Today,* Python Press 2013

Dean Radin, *Real Magic*, Harmony Books 2018.

Gail Reichstein Rex, *Earth Acupuncture*, Bear & Co 2016.

T. Edward Ross and Richard D. Wright *The Divining Mind,* Destiny Books 1990.

T. Edward Ross, *The Healing Mind,* American Society of Dowsers 2013

Samuel Sagan, *Entity Possession*, Destiny Books 1997.

Paul Screeton, *Quicksilver Heritage*, Abacus 1977.

Michael Talbot, *The Holographic Universe*, Grafton 1991.
 - *Beyond the Quantum*, Bantam 1988.

Nikolai Tolstoy, *The Mysteries of Stonehenge*, Amberley Publishing 2016.

Nigel Twinn, *Beyond the Far Horizon –The Life and Work of Billy Gawn*, Penwith Press 2012.

Websites

Dowsing Societies

There are many more than listed here – these are some that I have presented at, or have some relation with:

British Society of Dowsers
https://britishdowsers.org/

American Society of Dowsers
https://www.dowsers.org/

Canadian Society of Dowsers
https://canadiandowsers.org/

Canadian Society of Questers
https://questers.ca/

West Coast Conference (Santa Cruz - biennial)
http://www.dowserswestcoast.org/

South-West Dowsing Conference (Flagstaff - biennial)
https://www.dowserssouthwest.com/

Dowsers Society of New South Wales
https://dowsingaustralia.com/

New Zealand Society of Dowsing and Radionics
http://www.dowsingnewzealand.org.nz/

Japanese Society of Dowsing
http://dowsing.jp/english/index.html

Italian Society of Radionics and Radiesthesia
https://www.radionica.it/

Other websites of interest

International Dowsing Day
Annual event (5 May) celebrating dowsing.
https://www.facebook.com/internationaldowsingday/

British Dowsing
Discussion forum, EEG Glossary of Terms and Newsletter archive, Roy & Ann Procter's research and book.
https://britishdowsing.net/

Western Geomancy
Grahame's website, shop, and blog
https://westerngeomancy.org/

Adventures in Dowsing
The original internet dowsing podcast.
https://adventuresindowsing.com/

The Geomancy Group
Reference and listing of UK practising geomancers.
https://geomancygroup.org/

Mid-Atlantic Geomancy
Sig Lonegren's site. Great reference.
http://www.geomancy.org/

Notes and References

Chapter 1: Models, Magic, and Metaphysics

[1] *Science*, 13 June 2014. http://www.sciencemag.org/content/344/6189/1265

[2] Bird, Christopher, *The Divining Hand*, Whitford Press, 1993

[3] Philip Goff, *Galileo's Error: Foundations for a New Science of Consciousness*, Penguin 2019

[4] https://plato.stanford.edu/entries/panpsychism/

[5] 'The first principle is that you must not fool yourself and you are the easiest person to fool.' — Richard Feynman

[6] These thoughts on divination are adapted with permission from Ivo Dominguez Jr's book, *Casting Sacred Space*

[7] Aleister Crowley, *Magick in Theory and Practice (Book 3)*

Chapter 2: The Resonance of Water

[1] https://www.theguardian.com/science/shortcuts/2017/jan/31/guide-to-holographic-principle-of-universe

[2] https://en.wikipedia.org/wiki/Anthropic_principle

[3] For more details on the double-slit experiment, see: https://plus.maths.org/content/physics-minute-double-slit-experiment-0

[4] Leslie L Mooney, *Diversion of Underground Streams*, ASD Digest, Feb 1964

[5] From a workshop at the 2015 ASD conference.

[6] T. Edward Ross and Richard D Wright *The Divining Mind*, Destiny Books 1990

[7] T Edward Ross II, *The Healing Mind,* American Society of Dowsers 2013

[8] https://theamericanscholar.org/the-dowser-dilemma/#.VI3HM7_gXnM

[9] https://en.wikipedia.org/wiki/Water_memory

[10] Dean Radin, *Real Magic,* Harmony Books 2018

[11] Alanna Moore, *Touchstones for Today,* Python Press 2013

[12] Paul Screeton, *Quicksilver Heritage,* Abacus, 1977

[13] Nikolai Tolstoy, *The Mysteries of Stonehenge.* Amberley Publishing, 2016

[14] Rasmus Gaupp-Berghausen, *Sound of Soul* workshop, British Society of Dowsers Conference 2014

[15] Eliphas Levi, *Transcendental Magic*, trans. A. E. Waite Weiser 1968

Chapter 3: Geopathic Stress

[1] Christopher Bird, *The Divining Hand,* Whitford Press 1993

[2] Christopher Bird, *The Divining Hand,* Whitford Press 1993

[3] Käthe Bachler, *Earth Radiation - the Startling Discoveries of a Dowser*, Wordmasters 1989

[4] https://betweenrockandhardplace.wordpress.com/2014/10/18/former-nokia-technology-chief-mobile-phones-wrecked-my-health/

[5] Gardner, Grahame, *A Basic Guide to Technopathic Stress,* Western Geomancy 3rd edition 2018

[6] https://www.nasa.gov/mission_pages/sunearth/news/gallery/schumann-resonance.html

[7] Cherry, Dr Neil, *Schumann Resonances, a plausible biophysical mechanism for the human health effects of Solar/Geomagnetic Activity,* 2002

Chapter 4: Shamanic Cosmology

[1] Davidson, Hilda Ellis, *Lost Beliefs of Northern Europe*, Routledge 1993

[2] https://en.wikipedia.org/wiki/London_Stone

[3] For a more in-depth explanation of this model, see Farrar & Bone, *Progressive Witchcraft,* Career Press 2004.

[4] In the Southern Hemisphere, these associations are reversed.

[5] https://en.wikipedia.org/wiki/Salamanders_in_folklore

[6] https://en.wikipedia.org/wiki/Sylph

[7] https://en.wikipedia.org/wiki/Undine

[8] https://www.martycain.com/

[9] https://en.wikipedia.org/wiki/Active_imagination

Chapter 5: Ethics and Protection

[1] https://en.wikipedia.org/wiki/Barton%27s_pendulums

Chapter 6: Spirit of Place

[1] All five altars can be seen in Glasgow University's Hunterian Museum.

[2] https://en.wikipedia.org/wiki/Imbolc#Etymology

[3] https://www.zoence.co.uk/pages/landscape-temples.html

[4] Thanks to Gary and Caroline for allowing me to share this information.

[5] http://www.cheviotwalks.org/art2.html

[6] Originally published in Vol 59, no 1, Autumn 2019 issue of *The American Dowser*, the journal of the American Society of Dowsers.

[7] A version of this story appeared in the July 2012 issue of *Dowsing Today*, the journal of the British Society of Dowsers.

Chapter 7: Practitioner's Guide

[1] This is all-too-frequently used as an excuse by some dowsers when they don't find the results they expected!

[2] https://en.wikipedia.org/wiki/Flint

[3] Terry Pratchett, *The Wee Free Men (A Story of Discworld)*, Doubleday 2003

[4] https://www.bgs.ac.uk/opengeoscience/

[5] https://www.usgs.gov/

[6] As discussed in *Dowsing Magic – Book 1*. See Blanche Merz, '*Points of Cosmic Energy*', C W Daniel Co 1995

[7] https://en.oxforddictionaries.com/definition/curse

[8] https://en.wikipedia.org/wiki/Deva_(Hinduism)#Etymology

[9] (e.g.) Samuel Sagan, *Entity Possession*, Destiny Books 1997

[10] http://www.spiritrelease.org/

[11] https://en.wikipedia.org/wiki/Hephaestus#Hephaestus_and_Aphrodite

Chapter 8: Environmental Remediation

[1] See Twinn, Nigel, *Beyond the Far Horizon – Why Earth Energy Dowsing Works: The Life and Work of Billy Gawn*, Penwith Press 2012

[2] Cowan, David, '*Ley Lines of the UK and USA*', Adventures Unlimited Press 2013

[3] See my YouTube video: https://youtu.be/jqKxwyrm84o

Chapter 9: Practical House Healing

[1] https://en.wikipedia.org/wiki/Cahokia

[2] http://www.dowsingmapper.com/

Index

About the Author

Grahame is a professional dowser and geomancer specialising in geopathic and technopathic remedial work, and consulting on the creation of sacred spaces such as stone circles and labyrinths.

Grahame served as President of The British Society of Dowsers from 2008-2014. On retiring, he was awarded the BSD Award and a Life Membership for exceptional services to dowsing and the Society. He is also a member of the Canadian and American dowsing societies, a founder member of The Geomancy Group, and co-chair of International Dowsers, created with Susan Collins of Canada to foster greater links between European and North American dowsing communities.

Grahame is a regular guest speaker and workshop leader at international conferences, including those of the American, British and Canadian national dowsing societies, the Canadian Questers, Escola Nacional de Feng-Shui in Lisbon, the Italian Society of Radionics and Dowsing, the Japanese Society of Dowsing, the Dowsing Society of New South Wales, and the ASD West Coast and Flagstaff conferences. In 2014 he was gifted his native name 'Carrier of the Sacred Fire' by First Nations Elder White Eagle at the ASD convention. He and his wife Elspeth live in Glasgow, Scotland.

You can contact Grahame through his website at https://westerngeomancy.org